MT

C0-AJR-107

DA

fact

THE ART OF SINGING AND VOICE TECHNIQUE

THE ART OF SINGING
AND
VOICE TECHNIQUE

VIKTOR FUCHS

New Revised Edition

LONDON
CALDER AND BOYARS

FIRST PUBLISHED IN GREAT BRITAIN IN 1963
BY CALDER AND BOYARS LTD.
18 BREWER STREET, LONDON, W.I.

REPRINTED 1967

© THE AUTHOR 1963

MADE AND PRINTED IN THE REPUBLIC OF IRELAND BY
HELY THOM LIMITED, DUBLIN

DEDICATION

With profound gratitude I dedicate this book to the memory of my beloved parents who taught me to appreciate and enjoy art.

And to the memory of all great artists who, by their unforgettable performances, have enriched my life beyond measure.

Finally I dedicate this book to my dear students and their pupils—may they all learn to enjoy and enjoy to learn as I have done throughout my life.

CONTENTS

CONTENTS

CONTENTS

CONTENTS

The Publishers wish to acknowledge with thanks the technical guidance of Miss Cynthia Jolly who edited the author's manuscript on their behalf.

ILLUSTRATIONS

PREFACE

IT was indeed a pleasure for me to read the interesting book on voice production by Professor Viktor Fuchs.

I shall be delighted to put on paper my opinion of it as a singer. I feel that the book with its different specified chapters must be a great help to anyone studying or teaching voice. For the singing student's part, it will become his best friend when he works at home by himself without the advice and ear of his teacher. It will become his dictionary when he is in doubt and thinks perhaps he is doing something wrong. He only has to go and look up the chapter dealing with his difficulty, and Professor Fuchs will hold the remedy.

Now don't think that by reading this book you can become a singer on your own. If you want to be more than a household voice, you must get a teacher who is experienced enough to teach you, and knows how to advise you. A singing voice is as different as fingerprints, and the road you must take to develop is different for everybody. Only the physical functions are the same.

There is an old saying that there are no perfect teachers, only intelligent pupils, and there is much that is true in this. Only when a pupil is intelligent and has worthwhile material, can a serious teacher show him how and give him the right help. So select yours with care. If there is nothing to work with and no intelligence, there is no hope for your teacher or you. Therefore this book is also of great value to the teacher. It may show him the road to take in his approach so that the pupil understands what he is doing wrong and how to correct it.

I therefore recommend this book to old and new singers.

LAURITZ MELCHIOR

CHAPTER 1

TEACHER AND STUDENT

THE RESPONSIBILITY OF
THE VOICE TEACHER

' What nobler employment, or one more valuable to the state, than that of the man who instructs the rising generation?'

CICERO: De Divinations, 78 B.C.

'I like to teach because I learn so much from teaching.'

PABLO CASALS:
quoted from an interview with Howard Taubman, October 1958.

In so-called civilised countries every child is given basic training in reading, writing and arithmetic—regardless of whether he goes on to a university, a school of higher education, or leaves after the prescribed minimum of state education.

But when a student studies singing, whether for pleasure or for professional purposes, it often happens that he can rarely answer a simple question about it. This may hold good after years of study, and a successful career as singer or teacher. Even an established star may approach a reputable teacher and ask (as has happened to me) whether in inhalation the diaphragm goes in or out!

Why is this? Would someone who has driven for years be incapable of explaining which was the accelerator and which the foot-brake? Why can a child be taught to read and write, but not to develop his voice as a speaking and singing instrument, at least in such rudimentary matters as how to take breath? Why do well-known teachers hold such different opinions, whether they teach privately or in good academies of music?

The main reason is that in no country is there a single authority whose judgment on singing is universally acknowledged. Unlike any other branch of study, teaching singing can be practised in many countries without a certificate of proficiency. The situation is paradoxical. A school music teacher, chiefly concerned with choir training and class singing, has to pass strict examinations before he can teach. But by dint of clever publicity, a private teacher can set up in practice and work with an exceptional voice, which careful training could develop outstandingly. He may damage it or even harm it irreparably. Such a self-appointed king has never passed an examination in his life, and need never explain how and by what right he is teaching. Imagine a man who cuts ordinary glass having to pass difficult tests, but a man who cuts priceless diamonds getting away with no proof of craftsmanship!

Then again, people come to teaching from very different backgrounds. The first group intend to teach from the outset, but most have spent years becoming (or trying to become) singers, and use their good and bad experience to teach others. Some start teaching after a more or less successful career, others take it up because they have never realised their own ambitions. Both groups *can* provide good and even excellent teachers.

As most students study privately, it is impossible to get even a rough idea of how many people give and take lessons, but both are certainly on the increase. There are two main reasons:

1. Through records, radio, television and cinema, it is much easier than it used to be for young people everywhere to

hear all types of singing. Many are attracted by the glittering success of a few, others are eager to imitate the effects that some singers achieve in their performances (e.g. Del Monaco, Callas).

2. Paralleling the increased appetite for opera the desire to produce it is growing everywhere; schools and opera workshops provide more opportunities for young people who have trained voices.

What Makes a Good Voice Teacher ?

Apart from the ability to teach, it is essential to hear *objectively*, as well as *subjectively*, as singers normally do, to be able to diagnose what is heard. I would call this *analytical hearing*. This is the skill of recognising how a student is producing his sound, and of then applying the right remedy. It has to be inborn, but it grows with experience. It is as important as is exact diagnosis for a doctor, it helps a teacher to remove the root-cause of the trouble.

Good singers are often not able to teach because they lack this quality: while some have a double gift for singing and teaching from their early years, as young actors are sometimes talented for acting and producing. Coaches, who are generally unable to sing, often lack it. A further distinction has also to be made between teachers who can assist the unambitious, and those who can guide the talented to the heights of perfection.

Professionally Active Singers as Teachers :

I. Some professional singers are interested in teaching even during a period of successful activity in their chosen field. If they possess the above mentioned talent, of objectively and not only subjectively hearing, they may gain much in their own singing. *Docendo discimus,* 'we learn while teaching', as the Latin says. However, the deciding factor

is not whether and how much *they* succeed, they must—
as teachers—always realise that the student has to develop
along the correct lines.

II. Most singers have (or should have) more patience with
others than with themselves, especially in exercises. By
watching and guiding others, they are often reminded of
their own vocal needs. But a singer must examine his
motives very carefully before beginning to teach. His
general attitude is very important.

A characteristic case comes to mind. Many years ago, a successful member of the Vienna State Opera, whose musical and vocal
mentor I had been for years, asked me whether he should start
teaching while he was still active as an opera singer. 'Why not?'
I said. 'You know a great deal, you could do it. But I would
like to ask you one question. Suppose a young, handsome singer
came to you, looking as you did twenty years ago, with a voice
like yours when you started, more brilliant top notes, but not
your famous *mezza-voce*. After his first concert, the critics lament
that he has not got your mezza voce. He studies with you for a
year till he gets it. Would this make you happy?' The singer
became red and agitated. 'I don't understand you. This young
man has a good voice, he is young and handsome, what does he
want a mezza-voce for?' 'I'm afraid you wouldn't make a very
good teacher,' I told him, 'You are already jealous of a young
man who only exists in my imagination!'

The danger with active singers who teach is that they are sometimes like mothers, who are jealous when their daughters marry
handsome bridegrooms. The teacher has to feel like a responsible
mother, not like a baby-sitter who dislikes children and only
takes the job for the money.

This brings us to the financial motive, which also leads teachers
astray. A prospective teacher should ask himself, 'Am I interested
in this responsible profession for its own sake, or only in the

income I shall derive from it?' Few singers can save money from their 'good' years, particularly when we consider that an opera singer is old at fifty. Actors are in a better position. Octogenarians can appear on stage—playing octogenarians. The danger is that many singers use the teaching profession as a sort of old-age insurance. While nobody would wish to begrudge them the opportunity of making a living, one has to point out that young students have a right to the best possible care. I would like to quote the case of a lyric baritone, who in his twenties enjoyed immense success at a famous European opera house. He had a most beautiful voice, which he frequently abused in faulty singing, in spite of warnings from the critics. When he was about thirty his voice cracked in a way that could have been put right. Instead of making this effort, he accepted a leading position in a top-ranking conservatoire. He had such a fine name that many with promising voices came to study with him, and conductors recommended talented students. Pitying the early vocal *débacle* of an outstanding singer, they harmed the career of many a young student. Some managed to survive in spite of his bad tuition; others with less remarkable voices disappeared into oblivion. Few seemed aware that a singer, who had abandoned his career through ignorance of the fundamental rules of singing was certainly not a proper teacher. It is shocking that conductors and other discriminating musicians allowed themselves to be led astray out of pity for a foolish singer.

Assessing a Teacher

A young student can seldom judge a teacher objectively. It depends too much on his personal liking and whether or not he makes progress. If he gets on, he will call the teacher good, and if not, he is quite likely to accuse the teacher of his own failure.

How can a teacher's qualifications be properly assessed, and who can do so? A teacher is normally considered good if he can produce a good singer or, better, a couple of good singers. But this is an imperfect way of judging, since a teacher depends on the vocal material, talent and co-operation of his students. A violin teacher will be glad if his student has a good instrument, but it will please him more if the student is talented and works hard. In singing, the quality of the instrument matters much more than in other fields. What is more, a successful start depends on many chance factors, irrespective of the teacher's worth or the student's achievement. Appearance is an incalculable asset: a pretty girl with a lovely voice and a lively personality is half-way to success, even if her technique is far from perfect. Young singers come to the notice of important people by chance, or are lucky in meeting the right person to help them.

As in so many other walks of life, we only hear about the success stories, and not the failures. Important men have started as poor newspaper boys: nothing is heard of the numerous newspaper boys who remained poor and needy. Teachers who publicise the successes of their singers write these names in brass, and their failures are passed over in silence.

The best way to judge a teacher is to hear his students at certain set intervals. A good musician, such as the Head of a Music Academy, or the Professor of Music of a music faculty, a conductor or cathedral organist should be able to judge the quality of a teacher: whether he is able to do this depends on the need for increased knowledge of singing amongst educated musicians.

Charlatan teachers boast (in the words of the doctor in *Gianni Schicchi*) that 'none of their patients ever dies'. Even in good magazines and newspapers, it is possible to read charlatan advertisements 'high notes created in shortest time' or 'technically faulty singing will be corrected', etc. An honest teacher could never promise so much! Students should be on their guard. Such teachers never admit their inability to keep their promises. They say 'the student was on the verge of improving when he lost patience and left.'

It is very dangerous to apply an economic yardstick to the choice of a teacher. The slogan of many parents 'Let us try first with a teacher who does not charge too much, and if you are really gifted, we will look for a better one' can easily prove disastrous.

Improving the Standard of Singing

Every country should aim at improving its standard of singing by giving its singers the opportunity of studying with competent teachers. In other words, better singers need still better teachers. The only way is for good music schools to set out to employ the best possible teachers to educate the teachers. After all, this is what happens in other branches of study. Sometimes performers can stimulate other performers and so increase the demand and the supply of high-level performance. The impressive success of Van Cliburn, for instance, will stimulate many talented piano students who might otherwise be attracted to popular music. He filled the vast Hollywood Bowl twice in one week, a feat previously accomplished only by popular concerts attended by popular film stars! He may well urge on other performers, just as Paganini spurred on Franz Liszt when he was on the point of abandoning his piano career.

THE VOICE TEACHER
AND HIS STUDENT

'To have brought to fruition a remarkable talent is a wonderful sensation—because it is the greatest benefit which we are able to confer.'

GOETHE's last letter to Marianne von Willemer, written a few weeks before his death (1832)

Just as a healthy person never realises his good luck till he falls ill and needs a doctor, so many students and professional singers fail to appreciate the good work of a teacher till something goes wrong with their technique or their vocal apparatus. The teacher is wholly dependent on the sincerity and honesty of a student, for afterwards nobody can prove what was done by the teacher and what was due to the natural endowment and skill of the singer. A craftsman, painter or writer can show the results of his labours, and does not depend on the co-operation of others to anything like the same extent.

For obvious reasons the relation between a voice teacher and his student is much more subtle than other teacher-student relationships. Some voice teachers aim at a close personal relationship with the student—this makes it much more difficult for the student to judge whether the teacher is going in the right direction. Based on my experience I have always admonished my students who intend to become voice teachers themselves never to get into a close private relationship with their students: a teacher never should hear from a student as an answer to a question 'That is none of your business.' However sometimes, for human reasons, a teacher is involved in the private affairs of his students. I will mention two cases which came my way:

1. In Vienna shortly after the first war, I was teaching a pretty young soprano, who was extremely gifted in light opera parts. It was one of the few times I was able to advise a woman to become an operetta singer. When she heard my advice, tears rolled down her cheeks. Her story was sad. At seventeen, she had married a handsome officer in the Austrian Army, who had been badly wounded, and had to live with him in a home for incurable officers. Only after long arguments had he agreed to let her study. He swore to kill her if she tried to leave him and take up a stage career. My news had therefore plunged her into deep distress. We continued her lessons for several months until

one morning I was visited by an unknown colonel. 'The life of your young soprano is in grave danger' he told me. He was living at the same home as the husband. 'She came home late last night, and said she had been delayed at your studio, rehearsing for a student concert.' The colonel mopped his brow. 'Of course,' he said, 'I know she wasn't at your studio last night. But I also know he keeps a revolver under his pillow and is extremely jealous. When he phones in a few minutes, you must save her life—and lie.' We waited for the phone call. When it came, I was forced to give my word of honour that the wife had been rehearsing at my studio the previous evening.

I never heard from her again. I can only hope that my first (and last) broken word of honour was able to save her life.

2. Eddie Constantine, now one of the leading singers and film actors in France, even as a young man had a beautiful big bass voice; he studied with me in Vienna for two years, and won a medal in the International Competition.

One morning he phoned to tell me he had throat trouble, which he was treating with a gargle prescribed by a young doctor. Two days later he called and said he could not put on his shoes as his feet were swollen. I was very worried and went to visit him with my doctor. Constantine's tonsils were severely inflamed, and he had a slight case of dropsy, which accounted for his swollen feet. An immediate operation was indicated, but the doctor needed the parents' consent, as the boy was a minor. I accepted all responsibility, as I knew that the parents would tell me to do what I thought best. The operation was a success, and a few weeks later Constantine sang better than ever. Later, I worked with him in New York and was able to get him a job at the Radio City Centre. From there he went to Paris, where he became a star.

Teachers often have to decide how much time and effort to

spend on a student, whose resources are more vocal than financial. After all the Lord bestows on a young person either a good voice or a rich father! Exceptions to this rule are few in my experience. On the other hand, it is quite impossible for even a good teacher and a talented student to work successfully on only one or two lessons a week. If the teacher offers the opportunity of more intensive study, he must take the full risk. I know from experience that the teacher is generally the loser.[1]

Such contracts can bind a student to stay with a teacher even when he could learn more by working with another. Students often change their plans and their profession, girls marry and renounce a singing career; the teacher has to abandon his claims. Sometimes a teacher finances a favourite student and treats him like a son. His one wish is that his pupil may succeed. Small wonder he is unhappy if he is rewarded with ingratitude, as he is powerless to prove that he gave invaluable technical help. Although teaching talented poor students is always a gamble, I condemn teachers who shut their piano if the student has not brought the fee for the lesson—and I am sure most of my colleagues would agree. Such a teacher is a business man. Is singing on Sale or Return? What ought a teacher do if the customer does not pay? Take away his good head notes and his High C?

Even after forty years of teaching I am unable to advise younger colleagues how to act in such cases. There will always be generous teachers, and others who only see their own advantage. There will always be grateful and correct students, and others who are shoplifters at heart, who leave without paying.

WHEN TO START LESSONS

When is the right time to start studying? There is no fixed rule, as it depends on so many factors. Girls may start sooner

[1] Unless like Caruso's teacher Vergine, he resorts to the base trick of expecting 25 per cent of his students' income for 'five years of singing', by which he meant five years spent singing. Caruso would have had to pay until he had sung his last note. He managed finally to settle this case in a satisfactory manner.

than boys, for the simple reason that they do not have to undergo such decisive changes as boys, who should never begin until they are seventeen. A boy is often used in quasi-professional singing before he is ten years old, generally as a choirboy. He should stop singing as soon as there is any sign of a break in the voice. This usually occurs when he is between thirteen and fourteen. The choirmaster must insist that he stop singing until he is at least seventeen. Some famous singers insist that they never stopped singing during this period of change, just as some people were declared dead by a doctor, and then came to life again! Such incidents are exceptions and should not be used as examples. Caruso, Chaliapin—to mention two of the most famous— possessed very beautiful voices as boys and earned money from singing. But a good boy treble will not necessarily become a good adult singer. It seems relatively unimportant whether an adult singer had a good voice as a boy; what is essential is that during the period of change the voice is given *complete* rest.

Teaching a young man of seventeen needs great care. Strenuous exercises and dramatic arias must be avoided. That some young men of this age look stronger than those in their twenties is no guide, and a teacher should not jump to false conclusions because of it.

The problem is somewhat easier where girls are concerned, as they do not change vocally. The proper time to start depends on the degree of physical development, and also on the climate. Girls from southern and tropical countries mature much sooner than those from northern countries. In Italy some girl singers reach maturity before they are twenty—but they grow older sooner. Most teachers agree that it is risky to start teaching a girl before she is sixteen or seventeen. To start earlier she must be exceptionally well-developed and her throat examined by a throat specialist. Strenuous exercises should be avoided, and the emphasis laid on good head resonance and proper breathing. Most coloratura sopranos start at an early age with a teacher who has recognised their talent, and developed their head resonance. The younger the singer, the easier it is to develop agility. It resembles dancing, which is begun even earlier. A good early grounding often results in astonishing flexibility and brilliance, but little warmth.

A talented child (or her mother) reads of the early start of a big star, and naturally feels she could do the same. But a teacher should not encourage it. True, if he refuses, mother and child may go to a less scrupulous teacher, who will persuade them that there is no danger. He may quote great women singers who sang as children such as Henrietta Sontag, who sang minor parts at eight and made a fully-fledged debut at fifteen; or Adelina Patti, who made her debut as Lucia at sixteen at the Park Theatre, New York. He will say nothing about the many children who sacrifice their youth for a vain dream, and learn nothing useful for their later years. Nor does he often give the full facts about these exceptional cases. Patti grew up in an atmosphere of good singing. Both her parents were opera singers, and her brother was her first teacher. At the tender age of seven she saved her family from ruin, when the impresario of her parents' opera troupe went bankrupt. Standing on a table in the concert hall, she sang such difficult arias as *Una voce poco fa* and *Casta diva*, with all the embellishments she used later on, in her resplendent career . . .

As stressed elsewhere, teachers should never give an immature girl dramatic arias, or arias with big passages in the middle range. She should never touch the dramatic arias of Santuzza, Gioconda, Sieglinde, Brunhilde, etc., before reaching complete physical maturity. Great dramatic voices of both sexes are like flowers, which grow slowly, and need proper nurturing and profound understanding. Singing too early may cause the premature end of a career.

GENERAL APPROACH

'The teacher should take the student by the hand and lead him along a long corridor. When they reach the door, he should give the student a key—so that he can open it.'

TOSI

The Audition[1]

The first meeting between teacher and student is called an audition. It is best to let the student choose a song (or part of a song), regardless of whether the choice is a good one.[2] A good teacher will also ask for some notes and scales before giving his opinion. Some beginners may have nothing to sing, others may be too shy. A definitive judgment may be difficult, even for an experienced teacher. He is able to judge the quality, range and condition of the natural voice, but cannot know how the student will study or how the voice will respond. It is an old habit of mine to accept a student for a trial period—say two or three months. This is particularly necessary when a student wants to know whether or not to take up singing professionally.

Naturally plenty of teachers accept every student regardless of voice and talent. Others reject a person who wants to 'learn to sing his favourite songs'. Teachers need a fixed income and/or a strong sense of responsibility to feel free to select their students. Ideally, they should be willing to train a student they have accepted to the highest possible standard.

Napoleon used to say that each of his soldiers carried a marshal's

[1] In his interesting book on *Garcia, the Centenarian and his Time* (Wm. Blackwood and sons, 1908), M. Sterling MacKinlay relates how he went to Garcia for an audition, accompanied by his mother. She was a former student and a well-known oratorio singer. Garcia was already over 91 at the time. He listened to the young man, and then advised him to wait another year! MacKinlay did this, then worked with Garcia for four years. It seems to have been his habit to ask potential pupils to rest their voices for a time, if he thought their voices were overworked. (cf. Middle Register, p. 86.)

[2] I remember a young girl, Rose Bok, who later became a leading coloratura in Hamburg, Berlin, Wiesbaden, and the Metropolitan. For her audition piece she chose the prologue to *I Pagliacci*!

baton in his bag. It is difficult to predict the future of a student, particularly if he is very young. Caruso's teacher Vergine accepted him after two auditions, but gave him little hope, because his voice was so small. Yet there are cases which are clearly hopeless, and it is much better to give an honest opinion. Some teachers hold out promise for the future, knowing that others will accept the student, even if they do not. This is inexcusable. Some are convinced that a student has a beautiful voice, even though others think differently. They are blind to his defects, like a doting parent, and may well hear lovely qualities in a voice they want to teach.

It is unwise to advise a student to give up a job so as to have more time for study. Who is rash enough to prophesy that a student will definitely make a success of his career?

The Danger of Premature Classification

Many teachers label a student straight away as a 'dramatic' singer, or say that he has a 'dramatic' voice. This is apt to lead both teacher and student astray. Some pianists may become Bach, Beethoven or Chopin specialists, although they may play the music of other masters to perfection. But they do not start out by asking what sort of specialist to become. This emerges at a much later stage of study. In singing, even a greenhorn wants to be labelled.

Tape-Recording of the First Lessons

Some singers forget how helpless and ignorant they were when they appeared in the teacher's music-room for the first time. It is not a bad idea to make a tape or record during the first lessons: it would serve to remind singers how much they owe their teacher. Some will still be unimpressed, and continue to think they developed more or less automatically!

The Giving of Explanations

The student should be given technical explanations of a kind he can understand. Garcia[1] used to say to his students before they opened their mouths:

> 'If you don't understand something, ask me straight away and I will try and clear it up. Remember we must guide the emission of the voice with our brains. Once the note is sung, it is too late to correct the fault. We must know what is right and how to do it. That is the Secret.'

Many teachers have plenty of technical knowledge, but never check up on how much the student has grasped—let alone whether he is acting on the advice given. It is quite different from a clerk in a courtroom, who has done his duty when he has uttered the legal phrases and made the witness swear 'So help me God'. The witness may or may not have understood him, but a teacher has to be certain. (When I lecture on the teaching of singing, I always insist that each student submits a weekly *résumé* of what he remembers. It is most illuminating!)

Supposing a student sings this useful exercise

AY OO AY OO   AY   AY AY OO AY   AH   AY AY OO AY   AY

and complains of tension in neck and throat, the teacher will explain that this is because he is exaggerating with the lips. He

[1] Manuel Garcia II (1805–1906...sic!) was one of the greatest teachers ever known. He became famous as the inventor of the laryngoscope. His father, Manuel Garcia de Popolo Vicente (1775–1832) was an outstanding operatic tenor who created Almaviva in *Barbiere* (1816). Garcia I brought the first Italian opera company to the United States (1825) and appeared in all the leading tenor roles. His wife sang secondary parts, while his seventeen-year-old daughter Maria, later famous as Malibran, created a sensation in New York. She became a legendary singer (one beautiful theatre in Venice still bears her name) but died at the early age of twenty-eight. Her younger sister Pauline (Viardot-Garcia) (1821–1910) was a great singer and later an outstanding teacher. Manuel Garcia II appeared in his father's company in bass and baritone parts (*Leporello, Figaro (Barbiere)* etc.) but gave up singing at the age of twenty-five to devote himself to teaching, which he did until close on his 100th birthday.

should imitate the student and then sing it as it should be sung.

Beginners need constant supervision while they are singing exercises. A teacher can help as much as a ballet-mistress by working the exercises with the student, so that he is used as a model, and the student can be corrected without interruption. If a student starts twisting his mouth, the teacher can imitate him at once; the student will realise what is wrong and correct it. Much time is saved this way. Teacher and student need to be in close visual contact. Some teachers never watch a student—a great sin of omission. It is easy to contract bad habits while singing. Some sing with a stiff jaw, others frown, stare etc., or always look in the same direction. In exercises and first songs, a student needs to look at the teacher with the same naturalness as if he were talking to him. A bad habit can then be checked at the very beginning. Even some successful performers sing with a twisted expression or a fixed look: others will hold one hand to their ears, especially when singing high notes. Such habits do not occur overnight: they are generally acquired in the studio of some teacher who failed to notice when they began.

Checking up with the teacher: Students should be encouraged to check up on anything and everything connected with singing: e.g., the professional tips given by famous singers. Gigli, for instance, said in an interview some years ago that he liked to warm up his voice by humming. It is not surprising if a student takes this as gospel and starts 'humming exercises.' It would be wiser to have checked with his teacher first. Humming may be a good exercise for warming up the voice, *IF the student can keep his throat open*. But this is very difficult for any singer! A rich man might say 'It's better to pay cash for your car, otherwise you spend too much in interest' or 'Buy a Rolls-Royce—it will last longer.'

This is only a typical example: a teacher should give a student the feeling he is ready to explain anything a student wants to ask.

Misleading and False Explanations

Many so-called 'explanations' are proof of laziness or even of ignorance. 'Open your throat,' 'Don't press on your Adam's apple,' etc., help about as much as if a doctor were to say 'See that your kidneys function better.' A young society lady once asked me if she had to have a groove in her tongue before she began studying. Upon my startled request for more information she told me that she had taken three lessons from a teacher who had tried to build a groove in her tongue. Presumably he had read somewhere that good singing builds a groove and decided to insist on it as a starting-point! (it sometimes occurs *as a result* of good, relaxed singing).

Many teachers cite useless examples to describe where sensations should be felt, using their hands and arms for explanations. Phrases such as 'The note has to float on the breath like a ball on a fountain', etc., have no value at all, and gesticulations with hands and arms are equally meaningless. Silly gestures only prove that the teacher does not know how to guide the student properly, just as travellers use sign-language if they have difficulty with the language. A teacher wants a student to feel the same sensations as he does himself and takes desperate steps to describe them. *Instead he should hear what is wrong by analytical hearing, (q.v.) and find the remedy through the right exercises.*

Accompanying Exercises

A voice teacher who plays the piano well has, of course, a great advantage. It is not so much technical ability that he needs as much as a capacity to 'go with' the singer. He has to *feel* how to play. If he cannot, he has to employ an accompanist, but the best accompanist cannot do as much as a teacher can to influence a student *from the piano,* particularly by showing him where and how to take his breaths. He often does a great deal without saying a word. Then he must know how to play for each student:

not too loudly for a light young voice, but firmly and decisively for high notes, otherwise the student will lack the necessary energy to reach them.

He should beware of exaggerating musical accents, for a student easily gets the habit of pushing higher notes and may never lose it, even after years of singing. Supposing he has to accompany Rodolfo's aria in *Boheme,* he can guide the student to phrase it in two ways.

The climax of the phrase is at (xx) and not at (x). A tenor without good breath control easily pushes the first A flat, and therefore is unable to save sufficient breath to sing the phrase correctly.

Acoustics of Teacher's Music-Room

If it is empty and over-resonant, with bathroom acoustics, it may harm a student's development. He will get used to the huge sound he is able to produce and will be disappointed when he sings in less resonant rooms. Some erstwhile singers (women especially) have rooms crowded with furniture of all kinds, tapestry, carpets, etc. Rehearsal rooms tend to be over-acoustic, so that inexperienced singers try forcing when they sing on stage. They forget to place their voice normally, as they are hearing themselves in a different way.

Group Lessons only for Ensemble-Work

A serious teacher will never work with more than one student at a time in his studio: only those who do not discriminate between individuals work in classes. It is quite a different matter if well-advanced students work together on a duo or ensemble. But even then a teacher must keep an eye on them, in case they slip into bad habits when they sing together.

WHEN SHOULD A STUDENT PRACTISE ON HIS OWN?

The best way to decide this important question is to let a student sing uncorrected at a lesson, telling him to try and correct himself. Only when a teacher is sure that the student can do this should he be allowed to practise on his own. Otherwise home study may nullify what has been done in the lessons.

Some teachers give exercises to be practised right from the start, like piano teachers, forgetting that a pianist hears a wrong note straight away. A wrong note on the piano does not disturb the one that follows, as in singing. The piano student can see the keys he plays, but a singing student can only feel and hear the notes, and even this is not entirely trustworthy for reasons explained in *How a singer hears himself*. How can a total novice be expected to hear if a note is right, when even experienced singers find it difficult to hear themselves properly?

The old Italian master Tosi wrote 'If the pupil has defects, especially nasal singing, throaty singing or hearing, he should never sing without his teacher being present.' If he disobeys, a teacher should disclaim responsibility. The great Italian masters of the 17th and 18th centuries were able to keep their students under observation as they usually lived in their master's house. Even a daily lesson gives little time in which to influence a voice, as the instrument itself is much more used for talking than for singing. That is why even the best singers cannot master their instrument like a pianist or violinist.

The following rules should prove useful: the lighter the voice the more they should be observed.

1. A student should know exactly which exercises to sing and in what range.

2. Although high notes may be sung during lessons, they should not be attempted when a student is on his own.

3. A mirror should be kept by the piano to watch mouth position, facial expression and (most important) eyes. Home practice needs visual as well as aural control.

4. The first practice periods should never last longer than five minutes, two or three times a day; later, they may extend to ten minutes. A short period is unlikely to cause harm, even if a wrong note or two is sung. On beginning again, the notes will probably be better-placed. Even teachers often fail to spot wrongly-placed notes straight away; they are like a derailed train; the longer it travels, the more damage is done.

5. Ideally, practice should only start when a student can sing songs, arias, and operatic parts. It may be possible to speed progress, but it may harm more than help. It is better for a student to limit himself to breathing exercises (p. 72) which should be done ten times at first, and later increased to fifteen or twenty times.

THE GRAVE DANGER OF NOT GOING STEP BY STEP

When does a person, adult or child, take piano or violin lessons? When they are interested in learning to play the particular instrument.

When does a person take voice lessons? When they—or someone else—has discovered that he or she has 'a voice'.

Herein lies the essential difference between voice study and learning to play an instrument. Singing means making music with one's instrument, the voice. Only people who are basically musical should expect to achieve success.

Progress and success is possible for students with fine voices, provided that they work hard for an adequate period, step by step, under the guidance of a good and responsible voice teacher.

Let's think now of the first songs a teacher gives to a voice student. If the teacher has sufficient experience and authority, he will select a song which fits the particular abilities of the student, which is not too difficult to master, and which falls within the natural range of the voice. The voice teacher will seldom be able to choose in the manner of the piano or violin teacher, who has carefully selected pieces prepared in albums, graded according to the development of the student.

In this matter the instrumental teacher goes step by step. But what is the procedure in voice teaching? Even in cases in which the teacher intends to guide the student in a similar manner as the piano or violin teacher, he finds many more obstacles than his instrumental colleagues. The reason for this is easily understandable when we consider that it is human nature for many students to desire to master more difficult pieces than they are able to at the time. But attempts of this kind will never be as dangerous for an instrumental student as for the voice student, when these attempts are made privately and without the consent of the teacher. First of all, such untimely and premature efforts will certainly hinder progress, but more important, might damage the 'instrument' of the student. On the other hand, voice students, even young people with some voice and talent for imitating, are often able to sing, most presumptuously, arias and songs, before they begin to take singing lessons. An experienced voice teacher will learn how to treat these particular students; being stern and inflexible in each case is as unwise as always giving in. The teacher should never stop emphasising that an intelligent student will realise *it cannot harm the teacher just as it does not harm the physician when his advice is not obeyed.*

The more musically educated the students, and the higher their

final goals, the less danger exists that they will try to sing something that the teacher has ruled inappropriate for the present. It
is a pity that some voice teachers with insufficient background in
music and burdened with false pride present a student with too
difficult a song or aria. Such teachers and also the students have
to be reminded that *it is not WHAT we sing but HOW we sing it*.

Should voice teachers start a female student with the aria of
Mimi from Puccini's *La Boheme*? And what is wrong with this,
a layman will ask.

Many renowned singers are able to sing 'Mi chiamano Mimi' in
perfect style. It is a kind of musical narration, very original, most
beautiful, that needs a natural expression and a great vocal technique, changing from expressive tones in the middle range to
sweet, high tones. Not only vocally, but in its always changing
moods of narration and in its musical style, it is a very complicated
piece of music—Puccini wrote more than twenty different
musical notations within seventeen measures. It is certainly
excellent material, but not advisable for beginners.

Another favourite choice is the aria from *Madame Butterfly*,
which needs a full sounding middle and lower range, besides the
ability to show great emotion—all that we cannot expect from
a young girl with little experience.

In other words, voice students are often not prepared by musical
principles that start with simple forms and advance to more
complicated ones. The way that many students are guided is as
foolish as expecting a child to learn logarithms and algebra before
he knows simple addition.

If voice students are good musicians because of past instrumental
training (piano, violin, etc.), their musical study will not be
delayed since they have learned the necessary musicianship; harm,
if any, would be to the voice and its development.

If a voice student has neglected the necessity of going step by
step, he will probably overlook the importance of this fact when

he becomes a teacher. However, a person who is predestined to become a good voice teacher has to learn wisdom by experience, i.e., through his own faults as a voice student. Like the burned child who dreads the fire, he has to be very watchful that his students do not repeat his failures.

A gifted voice student is often able to imitate a much too difficult aria—at least to his own satisfaction. A voice teacher, who is really concerned with the final success of a student, has to know the most advisable way of stopping this; furthermore, if the student is seriously interested in reaching a high goal in his art, the teacher must admonish him *to go step by step.*

CHAPTER 2

WORK OF THE TEACHER PREPARATORY

HOW A SINGER HEARS HIMSELF

THE voice is different from all other instruments, because only its owner can 'play' it. Furthermore, it is strongly influenced by any change in its owner, whether physical or mental, direct or indirect. A teacher cannot demonstrate on the 'owner's' instrument. The student has to use his own, and imitate the 'model' sound produced by his teacher.

But that is not all. A teacher hears his 'model' notes differently from the student, and vice versa. Nobody hears himself as others hear him. Whether in speaking or singing, one hears principally through *bone* conduction, and only to a limited extent through *air conduction*. Others hear us exclusively through *air conduction*. In other words, the sound-waves produced in speaking and singing reach the listener's ears directly, while the person who makes them hears them:

    1. Through bone conduction, i.e., from inside the eardrums.

    2. From the outside, but only under certain conditions.

(To understand the sensation of bone conduction, hum a tune and feel the bones of the upper part of the mouth vibrating.)

That is why anybody, who hears himself for the first time on a tape recorder or record is surprised at the sound of his voice; he imagined it to be quite different. To hear his notes as others hear them, a singer should sing into a microphone *and* wear ear-phones.

It is generally impossible to hear one's voice when singing in an ensemble, because the sounds made by other singers are much louder than those one makes oneself. This sensation is felt particularly by opera singers. When the soprano in *Aida* sings in unison with the tenor, she can generally only hear the tenor's notes, which have to project to distant parts of the theatre. (Radames needs a strong voice, above all in his high range.) As Aida and Radames are a pair in love, they sing at least a part of their duo while the tenor embraces his partner. His sound waves come to the ear of his 'celeste Aida' from point-blank range, thereby deafening her own notes to herself—but not to him. Each of them hears the other more loudly than he can hear himself.

One may well ask: how can they sing if they can't hear themselves? Sooner or later opera singers acquire a certain skill in *feeling* their notes instead of hearing them. How could the soprano in *Aida* hope to hear her voice when she has to lead a huge ensemble? She feels the *placement* of her notes, and this has to compensate her for the hearing loss.

Bathtub Singers

Many singers, amateurs as well as professionals, enjoy singing in the bathtub or under the shower. It is easy to understand, because the bathroom is small and its tiles serve as excellent resonators. Then we depend not only on bone conduction but on magnified notes, which are sent back to our ears through the air because of the favourable acoustics. We hear ourselves far better than if we sang in a large room.

On the other hand, singing or speaking in a large room without good acoustics, or in the open air, is essentially dependent on bone conduction, and on our habitual sensation for each note, e.g. the vibrations we feel on a certain part of the palate. Singing in a vocal ensemble also depends entirely on this kind of control.

Sometimes even an experienced singer will hold a completely

different opinion about his singing from that of a conductor or coach. He may think that a particular note or phrase was quite good, while others prefer one which the singer actually disliked. I will quote two characteristic cases from my own experience:—

1. A leading tenor of the Vienna State Opera, who had studied with me for years, wanted me to hear as many of his performances as possible. One evening I arrived for a *Tosca,* and realised that my friend was in poor condition and did not sound as free as usual. But at the end of an act he sang two excellent high notes. As he was a favourite with the audience, I was surprised he took no curtain calls with Maria Jeritza. I hurried to his dressing-room, and found him in a very bad state. 'You know', he said 'I was so happy you came and found me in such a fine form tonight, but the last two high notes were so bad that I refused to take any curtain calls'. 'You're crazy', I told him. 'I was worried about you in the first act, but after those last two notes, I knew you had recovered because your placement was right.' The tenor was flabbergasted. It took me quite a while to convince him that in spite of his experience, a singer cannot always tell whether a note is right or not.

2. The second case concerns my first years as a teacher at the Vienna Conservatory. At that time I was frequently singing in concerts and oratorios, and appeared on and off as a guest artist in my old baritone parts. My successful work with coloratura sopranos, high tenors and baritones was giving me an opportunity to develop my high range which was becoming more and more easy. I decided to sing a tenor aria from Puccini's *Turandot* for a coming benefit concert. I invited five of my most advanced pupils to examine their teacher. I told them I would sing the aria twice, singing the B flat differently each time. They were to write down, independently of each other, which note they considered the better. It came out as I expected. All five wrote that the second B flat was the better, whereas I, as the singer,

felt just the opposite. As the teacher, I was right; the note I heard as a singer and thought the better was for them the less good.

THE BATTLE AGAINST
MISUSED MUSCLES

'Above all, let the nurses speak well. The boy hears them first and will try to shape his words in imitation.'

QUINTILIAN, Roman orator and teacher, A.D. 35-95.

How does a baby learn to talk? By imitating, often quite un-aided. His parents, and people round him, generally enjoy his first awkward attempts to communicate, and imitate him back instead of correcting him. How difficult it would be for an adult student if a teacher merely imitated his mistakes! But, worse still, a child learns incorrectly, because nearly all 'models' use their voices badly, both in production and pronunciation. Even teachers sometimes have a nasal twang, or speak with a regional accent or a dialect. Dialect in any language is the enemy of good speech and singing, because it springs from laziness. It is a kind of shorthand, since people who live for years at close quarters can understand each other without clearly-articulated speech. They write each other a 'brief note' instead of the 'formal letter' they would write someone living in another country or another city. In Brooklyn, N.Y., we hear *foist* instead of *first* because people are too lazy to form the *r*; in Naples *Chiusto* instead of *Questo*; in London, 'Gotta pinta milk?'

Generally what happens is that a child gets used to the dialect he hears at home, and retains it even when his teacher speaks well. The longer he is under its influence, the harder it will be to unlearn it. One need only think of Professor Higgins' efforts in

Pygmalion to make a lady out of a flower-girl by eliminating her ugly dialect and teaching her how to speak correctly. When each word is carefully formed, the voice sounds better too. Franklin Delano Roosevelt had a naturally good voice which sounded even better because he used it well; but even an ordinary school fiddle sounds better if Heifetz plays it.

With few exceptions, when something is done requiring muscular coordination, the nearest muscle-group is used; when children make their first attempts to write with pen or pencil, they tighten the muscles of their fingertips instead of using muscles that are further away. Most beginners in singing tend to tighten the nearest muscles (e.g. in throat or mouth), particularly when forming vowels and consonants. (Exercises for muscular relation are detailed in *Mouth position and Vowels and Consonants*.) Even good singers are often not aware how their tone-quality would improve, if they prepared the right muscles, particularly before singing in a higher range. How can a tenor sing 'I love you' on a high note, and show signs of strain in face and eyes! Strong harnessing of abdominal muscles should not involve the facial muscles. It is a matter of technique and routine, and we could learn much about muscular mastery by watching the classical dancer. In a *pas de deux* a relatively slight man can catch and hold his partner with one hand and keep the other moving gracefully. Both in dancing and singing we are dealing with art, not sport, which means that there must be no signs of strain anywhere.

THE NEED FOR A PROPER MOUTH POSITION

Giambattista Mancini (1716-1800) wrote in his *Practical Reflections on the Art of Singing*:

> 'The first fault comes when one draws out the voice without paying any attention to the mouth, and thus opens it

badly. At the first thought it seems that this fault is very easily corrected, but although this is the most common fault it is not easy to remedy. The first thing a teacher says to a pupil, is: OPEN YOUR MOUTH. And then he thinks he has fulfilled his duty. But he has *not*, in my opinion. It is necessary to explain, in a pleasant manner, to the inexperienced youth what is precisely the right position of the mouth, relative to his physiognomy . . . The rules for the opening of the mouth cannot be general, nor can they be made universally the same, for every individual does not open his mouth in the same way. Some have wide openings, some narrow and others medium. *Add to this the irregularity of the teeth.'*

And later:

'I have at last fixed a general rule: 'Every pupil must shape his mouth for singing *just as he shapes it when he smiles.* The upper teeth show a little, and are slightly separated from the lower ones.'

Another famous teacher, Pier Francesco Tosi (1647-1727) said the same thing in *Opinioni de cantori entichi e moderni o sieno osservazioni sopra il canto figurato,* 1723: 'The singer opens his mouth as if he were smiling.' Manuel Garcia II also held the same opinion in his *Ecole de Chant,* 1847 (English edition, edited by Beata Garcia, entitled *Hints on Singing,* 1895).

Good note placement always depends on the mouth position, and opening it too wide is as bad as closing it too tightly. Everyone's mouth is differently formed, and the teacher must discover the best position for each individual. It is obviously foolish for anyone to imitate the way another singer opens his mouth. Even as beginners, some students open their mouths easily: they may have a naturally wide mouth, with the front teeth protruding slightly over the lower, and keep this position when they sing. Such happy souls do not know the work they have been saved.

Their 'singer's mouth' is the equivalent of the pianist's long fingers. People whose upper and lower teeth meet equally, and especially those with protruding lower teeth, will always have difficulty, and will need to prepare their mouth position very carefully.

Many open their mouths with a slight jerk, the mouth being hinged near the ear. The teacher must demonstrate what happens, by opening his mouth smoothly without jerking, and singing a note with the right mouth position. He can then change the mouth to an incorrect position by pushing the chin forward— still sustaining the note. The student will hear at once how the note loses quality and brilliance. Most students stiffen the lower jaw, which is the equivalent of the stiff wrist of a pianist or violinist. It is a rule rather than an exception, just as novice dancers, especially older ones, are wooden in their movements. A beginner's exercises, like a professional's, always aim at reducing stiffness and substituting grace and smoothness.

A stiff jaw or strained mouth affects the tone quality and the smooth binding of notes. Like the tuning knob of a radio, a very slight movement can make the tone sound better or worse. Even a singer with perfect breath-control cannot sing floating notes unless the muscles round and inside the mouth are free of tension. The best exercise to eliminate tension is an extension of the demonstration described above. Using a mirror, sing any sustained note (its placement must be sure) and move the jaw slowly downwards without disturbing the free passage of the note. If placement is not secure, the exercise should be practised without singing, by simply exhaling slowly. This exercise is particularly useful for heavy voices. Moving the jaw while singing should naturally not become a habit: it is merely a check-up.[1]

A stiff jaw or tight mouth can be equally disastrous for facial

---

[1] This exercise can also be used with different emphasis to gain legato and head resonance (see p. 72, *Guardian Angels* ; p. 101, *Legato*).

expression. The tenor may be singing 'I love you', but to the audience he seems to be saying 'I hate your guts!' In these days of cinema and television, the singer cannot take chances. Facial expression is much more important now than it was when singers were primarily meant to give pleasure to the ear.

It is excellent advice to encourage a singer to smile naturally when he does his exercises, since everyone can smile, and does it in his own way. This position means that the chin cannot jut forward. It is possible to use this position for early exercises, and it can later be adapted for certain phrases or notes. The smiling position has the effect of thinning out the tone. It is essential for agility and for gay, fast music, and hence is the favourite of coloratura sopranos. It is also needed in *secco* recitative, and thus in Italian *opera buffa,* French *opera comique* and light operas of all sorts, unless the music is sentimental or sad. Some Italian tenors make the grave mistake of using it when they sing serious phrases!

The vowels AY, AH and EE should be sung in the smiling position. But Oh and OO (Ü) need the more mellow tone given by a rounded position, when the mouth is shaped into an exaggerated kiss. The starting-point for these vowels should still be the natural position of the mouth. The lips come forward, but not the chin: *only the lips should move.* (See VOWELS AND CONSONANTS, p. 51). In *secco* recitative the mouth-shape is adjusted to each vowel and consonant, as in speaking; but a legato phrase, particularly a high one, needs whatever shape is best for a good, smooth tone.

The smiling position has other advantages as well. Not only do the teeth look better in a smiling mouth, but they can act as resonators, and so enrich and beautify the tone. To cover the teeth with the lips is to lose on sound. Here a warning is necessary. Some students try to *imitate* a smiling position by LIFTING the upper lips. This looks not only unnatural, but hinders a smooth floating line. People with short upper lips and long teeth *always* show their teeth even if they are not smiling: people with short teeth and long upper lips do not necessarily show them even when smiling.

Children, boys especially, often open their mouths too wide in a choir, probably in the attempt to sing more loudly. Later they may become professional singers, and their exaggerated mouth-opening will persist in spite of energetic work by both teacher and student. In singing the mouth should never be opened to its fullest extent. Yet it can help as an exercise in cases of persistent jaw-stiffness, if it is practised as a slow smooth movement. Another good exercise for jaw-stiffness is to draw back both corners of the mouth as far as they will go without making a grimace. Keeping this position, the student should speak long phrases, slowly at first and then increasing speed. He should sing notes and phrases in the same way. The sound should remain the same when the mouth-position is normal.

All exaggeration should be carefully avoided. A singer who constantly smiles is as bad as the singer who always shapes his mouth like a fish. Basses and baritones often sing legato phrases this way. But a light soprano or tenor would be at fault if they sang a phrase up to top C with a round mouth! As most students tend to imitate the mouth-position of their teachers, an experienced teacher will often guess at a first audition whether the previous teacher was a bass or baritone. A good teacher ought to change his voice and his normal mouth-position, if his singing of any particular phrase does not fit the voice that he is teaching. It is a frequent cause of trouble.

One well-known baritone began to teach when he could no longer sing the great Wagnerian roles for which he was famous. During the early part of his career he had been a lyric baritone, and his voice had a very light colour. When he could no longer appear in lyric roles because he was overweight, he was forced to change to heavier, dramatic roles like Wotan, Sachs, etc. He had ample routine and volume to sing these parts well, but his voice was too light. He tried to darken it by singing with a round, protruding mouth. After a few years of this 'pseudo-technique' (q.v.), his voice started to deteriorate, and he retired. His reputation and connections won him a position in a reputable music school. Unfortunately, he was so accustomed to this mouth-shape that he used it to demonstrate exercises to young girls. Small wonder that they made a strange impression when they sang their light-hearted songs with such an unnatural look!

Jaw stiffness often affects opera singers who have been singing for years in Wagnerian and other grand operas, so that they habitually sing high notes as if they were blowing a trumpet. Sooner or later these notes may become fixed and shrill, and the singer will be unable to sing a real Wagnerian *cantilena*, let alone the smooth legato needed for Italian roles. Admittedly, such notes are effective in heroic roles. But to keep their beauty, a singer should always be able to crescendo through them. 'Electric bell' notes, which are heard from some coloratura sopranos are also the result of a stiff jaw.

Some singers, opera singers particularly, may sing with a wry face in spite of many other good qualities. I remember two excellent singers at the Vienna State Opera. One was a baritone who sang villains, as baritones frequently have to do, and developed a face-twist towards the left. There was also a bass who constantly opened his mouth to the right. The producer, a friend of mine, was not sure how to have them sing a *duo*. A difficult question!

A student may ask how a well-known singer falls victim to such a habit. It is much simpler than one might think. The more important the singer, the less inclined is a conductor or producer to try and check a bad habit, so that it is much more difficult to get rid of it. Another bad habit is always to look in the same direction when singing high notes. Once I agreed to work with a leading soprano at the Vienna State Opera, who was often corrected for this. Fortunately she was not yet well-known, and was intelligent enough to accept tactful suggestions. When she sang her head always leaned to the left. It was unpleasant to look at, and both she and the conductor realised that her notes were suffering from the rigidity, not to mention the difficulty she had in singing a love *duo* with her partners! The lover (tenor) always had to stand on her leaning side!

I was unable to correct her till I discovered the reason. I watched her while she was studying a part with her coach, and realised that she always sat on the right side of the piano bench, and leaned her head to the left when looking at the score. Being young and musical, she had studied many parts as an understudy, sitting for hours at the piano. Once the cause of the trouble had been found, it was not difficult to find a remedy. I made her sit on the left side! All the same, she had to work very hard to break herself of the habit.

The moral for both teachers and students: discover the right mouth position in time . . . and check up on bad habits!

CHAPTER 3

BUILDING THE INSTRUMENT

FIRST STEPS

'He that climbs a ladder must
begin at the first rung.'
WALTER SCOTT, Kenilworth VII

First steps are vitally important. A bad beginning on another instrument does not have such fatal consequences. A piano teacher starts off with a well-tuned piano, whereas a singing teacher has to build and tune the instrument before he can teach a beginner how to use it.

Admittedly, some untrained voices are almost perfect within a limited range. The task is then to transform a natural perfection into a conscious mastery. Otherwise it might for some reason be lost, and there would be no hope of regaining it. Yet natural and untouched voices such as these are relatively rare. Most students have tried to sing before they begin studying.

The primary concern with the voice as an instrument-in-formation is the reason why a teacher cannot concentrate systematically on improving a student's musicianship, as an instrumental teacher can. For the same reason a student cannot work for hours by himself as an instrumentalist can (see 'When can a student practise on his own?').

The first lessons are concerned with breathing, opening the mouth, avoiding a stiff chin (see relevant chapters), and with learning to sing several notes in the middle of the range.

4

Range: What is the best range for the first lesson? What is the right note to start on in exercises? Experience has taught me that it is best to start on:

Male voices

(tenors)

(baritones)

(bassos)

Female voices

are often more complicated, even when the student has not studied before. Generally I begin on

(sopranos who have never studied)

(girls with deeper voices who have sung with a forced chest register— whether they know it or not.)

It is advisable, in the latter case, that the lower range is avoided during the first lessons. During these lessons work should be concentrated on developing a good head resonance.

The first stage is reached when vibrations begin to be felt on the palate (see Resonance in Singing and Speaking): the second when a whole series of notes can be sung with a similar sensation on the hard palate. The higher the note, the more this will change (see Diagram in chapter 'Covering and Colouring'). Legato (or the smooth linking of notes) is studied from the first lessons.

(See Legato, p. 101.) Insert exercises which link 2-3 notes in easy compass, no words, small intervals.

First Stages in Teaching Lower Voices

A deep voice (which may develop into a dramatic soprano, mezzo-soprano or contralto) will come to no harm if all notes,

from to

are taken like the upper register in the early exercises. Lower notes normally belonging to the chest register can be sung with a great deal of head resonance mixed into the middle register. The teacher must decide when real chest notes must be sung (see 'Chest Notes', p. 89).

VOWELS AND CONSONANTS

'Without good pronunciation the singer robs the audience of an important part of the charm which words give the songs. If the words are not distinctly spoken, the audience finds no difference between the human voice and the sound of an instrument such as a horn or an oboe. Singers should not forget that they have words which elevate them above instrumentalists.'

TOSI (1723)

The voice is a most difficult instrument to train because it is concerned with more than notes. The singer has three obstacles to overcome which do not exist in other instruments:

1. Sung notes are based on various vowels, often used incorrectly in daily conversation.

2. The sound-waves are often interrupted by consonants, which also tend to be incorrectly produced.

3. A singer influences tone emission through verbal expression. This is not the same as the musical phrasing.

Meticulous study of vowels and consonants, like voice placement, is of vital importance. The student has to feel he is learning a new language: the more he feels this, the better the results will be. It is up to the teacher to decide how long the period of singing without using words continues, but generally speaking, the longer the better. In any case, he should continue until the throat feels free and relaxed, and the mouth and neck muscles in no way strained.

The vowels used in singing have a twofold importance:

1. *To unify tone.* Every vowel has its own sound, based on the right use of the muscles concerned. By singing or speaking a linked series of vowels, unified tone colour can be obtained. (See exercises on p. 54.) A series of correctly sung or spoken vowels should never be followed by an incorrectly formed series, as this impairs the floating sound.

2. *To assist voice placement through good vowel combinations.* Vowels are the best, if not the only way of influencing voice-placement; the teacher has to find the right vowel-combinations to achieve this, and the success of his teaching depends on his skill in selecting them. They are known as 'auxiliary vowels'. (Pure vowels are the final goal, but in most languages, except Italian and Russian, they are mixed.) For instance, a teacher may recommend the auxiliary vowel AY (as in Pay) (*a*) to extend the higher range, and (*b*) to teach head resonance. Or he may recommend darker vowels to make the voice more mellow (e.g. OH and OO). The meticulous mixing of note colour in singing is as essential as the mixing of colours in painting. Laymen seldom guess the exact colour-mixtures that painters have used,

and an audience only hears the general effect of skilful vowel
combinations. Sometimes the sheer fact of *thinking* of a darker
or lighter colour will influence a note advantageously. Con-
sciously or unconsciously, many great singers often use these
'auxiliary vowels' particularly AY on high notes.

The first exercises consist of notes with correctly-formed
vowels, and I recommend A as in ANTHONY excellent to begin
on, it is easy to relate to other vowel-sounds, as well as being good
for head resonance (see above). It helps to give the student the
feeling of placement, which he first feels as a vibration on the
hard palate. How long this will take depends on the extent to
which faulty amateur singing, incorrect speech habits, etc., have
created special problems. This is the first step in singing, just as a
piano student 'discovers' the key of C. The student should get
used to this sensation in the middle range before going any
further. The vowel can then be changed from A to AY as in
pay and later to AIR as in affair, by opening the mouth as for a
yawn. The sensation should be similar but not identical. Lesson
by lesson the student will feel a more intensive vibration on the
palate. The vowel AH (as in fast) can then be added at approxim-
ately the same place. It is good to let the student sing exercises
in which AY, AIR and AH all occur. At the beginning, they
should be sung as follows:

In other words, at this stage AH should not be sung on accented
notes.

The next step is relatively easy; A should be changed to EE,
but only in the middle range. (To sing EE on high notes is
difficult and dangerous even for experienced singers. As usually
sung it disturbs the vowels that follow. The mouth should not
be clenched, but half-open, in a natural way, as when smiling.)

With some students, a teacher may try for AH first, and other vowels later or vice versa. Or he may try the vowel OO, or better the French *U* or German *Ü* as in French *perdu* or German *Mühe*. This is difficult for English speaking students, who tend to sing OO until they are taught to form the mouth into an exaggerated kiss or whistle as they sing A.

The student then learns to sing all sorts of variations, in which the vowels change as well as the intervals:

Certain vowels tend to be better placed than others; the teacher has to find the right exercises for each individual, placing a 'bad' vowel between well-placed ones. Suppose AY, as generally happens, is already well-placed and AH is not, the following exercise will help:

Never sing 'bad' vowels on accented notes.

The singing of complete songs should not be allowed until 'bad' vowels are more or less eliminated, i.e., all vowels have a similar placement. Even one incorrectly-placed vowel interrupts the floating of the sound-waves.

The vowel-sounds have now to be unified, i.e., they have to acquire a common sound without losing their individuality. The simplest way is again the vowel A, which links all the vowels together homogeneously. A thus becomes a 'parent' vowel, as Lilly Lehman recommends in her book.[1]

[1] *Meine Gesangskunst* (How to Sing). This book contains a wealth of precious advice but is not easy for the average student to understand, particularly when she describes her sensations. The best parts are those which describe the incredible effect of well-placed head-notes. I owe to Lilly Lehmann most of my knowledge of women's voices and the blessing of head-notes, not to mention *piano and pianissimo!*

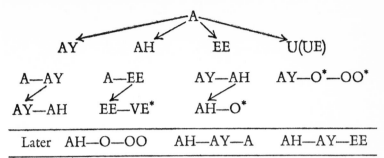

*O—UE—OO will be built by protruding the lips to an exaggerated kiss formation.
CAUTION : Watch the CHIN. Never protrude it.

It does not matter if auxiliary vowels can be heard during exercises. But in songs and in public, the listener should only hear the pure vowel. If the auxiliary vowel is audible, it means it has been exaggeratedly used.

Even when vowel-placement is homogeneous, perfect legato may still be endangered by certain words or syllables, which disturb the musical line and interrupt the sound-waves. (e.g. the word 'the' when singing in English.) Good singers know how to reduce the sound of these without breaking the line. After Richard Wagner had finished the long rehearsals for his *Ring der Nibelungen*, he wrote in a letter to the cast: 'Please, do watch the small notes, the longer ones come by themselves.' The small words need watching too!

With the pronunciation of words comes the second big obstacle: *the consonants*. All consonants must be produced with the right muscles: they too should never interrupt the 'floating' of the notes. The more 'dramatic' the way of singing, the more important the consonants, and the greater the danger to the voice.

Vowels should not be influenced by the coming consonants. For instance, in Aida's first aria:

a singer should do nothing about the following *N* while she is holding the A flat.[1] It should be pronounced with the *D* of the next syllable: 'Ndamor' and not 'damor' should be sung. This rule is even more important in languages such as English and German, which have many accumulated consonants. They should be grouped together in clusters.

Good singing depends greatly on the correct use of consonants. But their study should only begin when voice-placement is sure, and a melodic line can be 'sung' properly. Distinct articulation uses tongue and/or lips according to the particular consonant. But if a singer tightens his tongue for some vowel, or stiffens chin and lips when he sings a certain note, trying to articulate more distinctly will only aggravate the tension. A teacher or coach does more harm than good by telling a student to 'articulate more distinctly'.

It is obvious that Italian is the best language for singing, and English one of the most difficult. This does not mean that all Italians sing well and all English badly. Even Italian presents obstacles to singers who originally spoke an Italian dialect. But English-speaking singers have to work harder at overcoming the complications of their language (e.g. the tendency to a stiff jaw and insufficient lip-movement in forming each vowel): that they succeed is proved by the many good and even excellent singers of American and English origin.

As Giambattista Mancini (1716-1800) puts it in his *Pensieri e riflessioni pratiche sopra il canto figurato*: 'It cannot be denied by any nation that Italian is the most harmonious, softest and sweetest of languages. However, the Italian meant is clear, perfect Italian, the Florentine tongue. All other dialects, although Italian, are

---

[1] It seems traditional to sing the triplet out of time with a slight *ritenuto*. The A flat should not be longer than the other two notes of the triplet. An even worse tradition in this aria is frequently heard on gramophone records: the following phrase is sung as follows: although the accent is obviously on G and not on A flat, a second accented A flat is added. This is clearly not what Verdi intended, and breaks up the phrase for the sake of a breathing-space.

not suitable for the theatre because they lack accent and hence have not the melodic sweetness which is characteristic of pure Italian. The dialects are not so well adapted to music, because of their divided sound; one vowel will often have more than one sound.'

Poor Mancini! What would he have said to the many dialects and 'divided sounds' (i.e. diphthongs) of English? When Italian masters began with exercises on 'do, re, mi, fa, sol, la, si, do', the student always had pure vowels to sing. But in English pure vowels are rare, and even rarer in Oxford English! An English student who goes to Italy to study breaks away from the difficult speech-habits of his language by trying to use pure Italian vowels in speaking as in singing. Compare the words 'How do you do' with 'Buon Giorno', or 'How are you?' with 'Come sta?' when spoken by ordinary people. Even an ordinary Italian opens his mouth to say them, whereas a man who overpronounces vowels in English is clearly a foreigner!

The differences can be tabulated:

ITALIAN:

1. Has many unmixed vowels.
2. No diphthongs.
3. No accumulated consonants.
4. Many words begin and end with a pure vowel.
5. Liaison of adjacent vowels (a gift for the singer).

ENGLISH:

1. Has few pure vowels.
2. Many diphthongs.

3. Many accumulated consonants.
4. Very few words begin and end with a pure vowel.
5. Many words end with one or more consonants.

Duo Aida-Radames, Act III:

Admittedly there are many better English translations than this, but even the best translator is often at a loss to find English words without two or more accumulated consonants.

A useful tip about pronouncing diphthongs in English is given by an experienced English actress:

> 'Vowel sounds in English prove a stumbling-block to native and foreign singers alike, but if we turned all our diphthongs into pure vowels we would sound like foreigners. In diphthongs it is helpful to hold the first vowel till the last possible moment, and bring the second vowel to the final consonant.'

This is why it is better to begin by singing songs in Italian, and to postpone battling with English vowels until real mastery has been achieved. Italian arias too should first be learned in the original, so that the advantages of Italian can influence the English version without distorting its characteristic sounds. English-speaking singers will naturally feel envy for their Italian colleagues who with few exceptions are not expected to sing in any language other than their own.

Opera in English

For years there have been discussions about singing opera in English, both in England and in the United States. Competent connoisseurs like the late W. J. Henderson in his most informative book, *The Art of Singing* (Dial Press, New York, 1938) went so far as to claim 'We have some singers who can enunciate, but the typical American singer cannot sing his own language so that an audience can understand him. Opera in English is a lamentable travesty.'

There are, of course, a multitude of others who claim the very opposite. The vast majority of singers other than Italian and French often master other languages better than their own simply because they have to LEARN how to pronounce them, whilst in their own they find it hard to lose their ingrained bad habits. Critics often say they can understand singers in musicals, but not an opera singer when he sings in English. This is easy to counter. The less singer and public expect of the art of singing, the less difficult it is to pronounce well. The melodic line of a musical is not nearly so complex as that of a classic, nor is its range so wide. What is more, in popular singing, words attain more importance than melody. Singers in light operas, operettas, musicals, etc., generally steer a middle course between art-singing and popular singing: the 'lovers' sing as best they can, and the comedians entertain. Good operetta singers in continental opera houses generally need the same meticulous training as an opera singer, and must also be talented in acting and speaking.

The language battle is clearly not a matter for the singing teacher. His job is to teach his students how to sing English so as to overcome its notorious obstacles, and encourage them to master correct pronunciation. A well-trained singer must be able to sing correctly in any language.

RESONANCE IN SINGING AND SPEAKING

Resonance is essential to any instrument, but in the vocal instrument its mechanism is far more complicated and subtle than in man-made instruments. The piano has a wooden sounding-board, which enlarges and beautifies tone: the player merely presses down the pedal. The sounding-board of a violin or other stringed instruments is not so complicated for the player as the sounding-board of the voice. In singing, it depends entirely on the singer's skill how much the various parts of the human sounding-board react; very few people have naturally good resonance, and most have to learn how to develop it.

The singer and speaker can use as resonators the throat and mouth, nasal and head cavities, and the chest. A student has to learn how to place his notes so as to enlist the help of all parts of the human resonator.

How do they come into action? In speaking, most people use palatal resonance, so it is not all that difficult to use it in singing. The formation of the mouth can help a great deal. Whether the nose cooperates depends not only on facial formation, but also on the placing of the voice. In French the vibration of the nasal cavities is much more audible, and French singers feel that their nose is an essential part of their singing apparatus. Jean de Reszke, whose second language was French and who generally sang in French, went so far as to claim that singing is *only* a matter of the nose. What is certain is that its cooperation should always be passive and never active. Some degree of nasal resonance is essential, but as soon as it is heard, a singer may be sure he is using too much. It is like salt in scrambled eggs: it is obvious if there is not enough, but if it can be tasted, then there is too much.

Many people unconsciously exaggerate their nasal resonance, when it is known as 'twang'. Generally 'twang' is only a bad habit springing from imitation: children and teenagers often imitate a teacher or other person. It may also be traced to an abnormality of the nose, such as a swelling of the nasal mucous membranes or a too narrow dissection of the inner part of the nose. Parents should consult a specialist if they hear their child speaking in an exaggeratedly nasal way. A singing teacher should also recommend medical examination, as it is a habit which can jeopardise the beauty of the tone, if not damage the voice.

It is easy to test for *chest resonance*, and worth doing from time to time. A vibration can be felt if the hands are laid on the upper chest. If a phrase is sung which begins in the middle of the voice and leads on to higher notes, the chest vibration can be felt to stop as the higher notes are reached. Basses who play priests (e.g. Sarastro in *Magic Flute*, or Ramphis in *Aida*) often put both hands on the upper chest when they sing solemn phrases. This is not so much a devotional gesture as a check for chest resonance! Unfortunately, there is no such simple method of checking for palatal or head resonance.

A vibration should be felt on the hard palate of the mouth when singing or speaking notes in the middle range: public speakers too should always feel *palatal resonance*. This is the meaning of the widespread slogan 'Speak and sing in the mask'. But it is useless to expect it to function for the higher range, and an error to apply it by force to high notes, which have quite another sort of vibration. A bass or baritone may perhaps use the same placement for his whole range, except for his high notes, so that he always feels the vibration at the same place in his mouth. But he would be under pressure were he to sing higher notes in the same place, and he would have a limited upper range if the placement were to remain unchanged. All other singers will find it quite *impossible* to use the same note-placement for the higher range.

The higher the note, the more *head resonance* should be used: it means that the skull-cavities are vibrating. There is no rule about acquiring it. Some singers have it naturally, some learn it easily and quickly, while the majority learn it slowly and laboriously.[1]

Although it is possible to feel exactly where chest resonance starts and stops, no such sharp division exists for other types of resonance. Even in his middle range, a good singer enjoys the co-vibration of head resonance, and the transition to the so-called 'unmixed head notes' (those sung with almost 100 per cent head resonance, as only heard from good high sopranos) comes gradually.

Some singers have more resonance than others because the flow of breath within throat and mouth is not impeded in any way. There are several reasons for lack of proper resonance:

1. When notes are forced (resonance, like good acoustics or echoes, can never be achieved by violence);

2. When the throat and neck muscles are tight;

3. When the breath is not controlled.

A singer who masters all the possible resonances of the human voice carries his own microphone about with him wherever he goes.

THE REGISTERS OF THE VOICE[2]

A register may be defined as a series of consecutive, homogeneous notes which are produced in the same way and by means

---

[1] See *Guardian Angels—Head Resonance* for how to acquire it: also *High Notes*.

[2] Dr. Paul J. Moses, a most competent medical and vocal specialist of the Stanford University School of Medicine, writes of registers in his book, *The Voice of Neuroses**:
'How registers function may be seen with the stroboscope, unfortunately under the unnatural conditions obtained during mirror laryngoscopy. In singing the highest tone possible down to the lowest, the untrained singer first passes a sequence of tones of a different character. Then he comes to a "node", a switching point, from which he continues with a sequence of tones of a different character. Then he again reaches another "node" and switches to the lowest third of the range produced in a specific tone quality. The trained singer does not reveal these "nodes", since he has learned to unify the head, the middle and the chest register.'
* Grune & Stratton, New York, 1954.

PALATAL AND HEAD RESONANCE

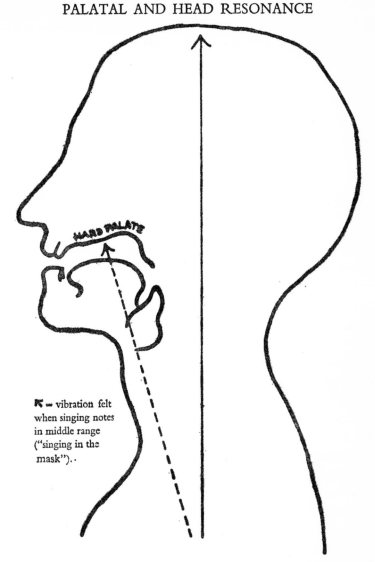

↖ = vibration felt
when singing notes
in middle range
("singing in the
 mask"). ·

↑ = (1) feeling of active **head resonance**. In good singing this should always *co-vibrate*.
It spreads around the whole skull and often makes the singer feel dizzy. (2) " Unmixed
head notes " use ↑ vibration without any vibration on palate ↖ (e.g. pp notes in Ave Maria
(*Otello*), Addio (*Traviata*), Requiem) (3) Notes above high C & D should **never be**
sung *ff* but sound like **flagiolet** on a **violin**.

of the same mechanism. Most teachers and singers now believe that both men's and women's voices consist of three registers—chest (lowest), middle, and head (highest).

Until Garcia invented the laryngoscope in 1865, all great singing teachers claimed that there were only *two* registers. Giulio Caccini (1546-1618), composer and singer, wrote in his *Nuove Musiche* about two registers of the voice, *voce piena* (full voice) and *voce finta* (disguised voice). He presumably meant the chest as full voice and the head as disguised voice. In 1613 the music theorist and chapel singer of Philip I and Philip II, Domenico P. Cerone, mentioned in his work, *El melepeo y maestro, tractado de musica theoretics y practica*, that there were two registers, chest and head. And Giovanni Battista Mancini (1716-1800) and other great Italian masters believed in the two registers, chest and head. At the time of his invention Garcia himself believed there to be only two registers. Only at a later stage of his teaching career did he break away from the traditional view, and assert that there were three registers, chest, middle and head.

As to the idea of 'one register' for the whole voice, there is no better explanation than that given by Professor Franziska Martienssen-Lohman, who writes in her book *Der Wissende Sänger*[1] (The knowing Singer): 'We can never accept "one register" as a fact in itself. Therein lies the fatal mistake which has already caused many victims among young singers through their ignorance of the natural limits of the registers. *One register is not a starting-point, but a goal.*'

When a singer changes from one register to another, he is like a driver changing gear. Obviously some singers will insist that they are not changing: such happy creatures are like drivers with automatic gear-shift. That does not mean there are no gears anymore than that there are no registers. A singer who neglects them or is unaware of their existence will run into trouble sooner

---

[1] This is a highly competent and enlightened book on the teaching of singing.

Lauritz Melchior
in and out of
costume

Professor Fuchs in three different roles

or later. How soon depends on how extensively he uses his voice, but a break will normally be the first sign of his negligence.

The truth of this can be proved by the following example; is it conceivable for a contralto or mezzo-soprano to sing the following two phrases in the duo between Aida and Amneris in a similar sound, or better with the same register?

Singing these two phrases reminds one of the beginning of the rondo in Beethoven's violin concerto. It is obvious that the violinist has to play the first part on the G string

and the second part on the E string.

Julius Stockhausen (1826-1906)[1] wrote: 'The registers in the human voice sound differently. Even the registers in a single voice often sound as if they were sung by different people.'

[1] Julius Stockhausen, pupil of Manuel Garcia and famous Lieder-singer. He gave the first public performances of many Lieder cycles (*An die ferne Geliebte, Die schöne Müllerin, Winterreise, Dichterliebe,* and songs by Brahms). Brahms accompanied him on one such occasion. He was an outstanding teacher, and Johannes Meschaert was one of his pupils.

A singer who blends the notes of different registers has an advantage over the string-player, who can only overcome the difficulty by *colouring* each note as much as possible in the same way. A singer on the other hand can *mix* the qualities of another register into the notes he is blending. In other words, he can mix head resonance into notes, provided that he has mastered this most precious register. Manuel Garcia II wrote in *Memoirs sur la Voix Humaine* (Paris, 1840): 'Head resonance does not necessarily begin where the chest voice ends, and a certain number of notes can be produced in either register.' It is wise to mix in the head register for special effects, and for blending. It is always dangerous to do the opposite, i.e. to ascend with the lower register to the higher one.

Professor Martienssen-Lohman remarks in *Der Wissende Sänger*, quoted on p. 64.[1]

> 'Head resonance can and must be added to a mixture in any range and volume of the voice. It is able to unite the sounds of notes. It is the "oil" for the entire activity of the registers.'

The rest of this chapter fully endorses this excellent comment.

The middle register is the most vulnerable (see relevant chapter 3). The more precious the voice, the more vulnerable, since it is used in daily life for speaking and for most singing. The range between 𝄞 and 𝄞 in young girls' voices is always weak. It is a sign of maturity when these notes sound full and expressive; after the age of fifty they are the first to lose power and mellowness. Some young girls try to compensate by colouring and straining—a most dangerous procedure. Singers in their late fifties on the other hand may be able to overcome the weakness by mixing in head resonance.

The chapter 'Chest Register' describes how the female chest

[1] Professor Martienssen was a student and assistant of Johannes Meschaert (1857–1922), the great Lieder-singer and teacher. The excerpts are quoted with her permission and that of her publishers, Atlantis Verlag, Zurich and Freiburg, Breisgau.

register is quite different from that in men's voices. The male chest register merges almost imperceptibly into the middle register, while the female chest register, like falsetto, cannot be assimilated to other registers. (The notes can always be sung in the middle register.)

In men's voices, it is relatively easy to get more sonority into the voice through colouring and mixing. A good baritone, for instance, may sometimes sing phrases of a bass or tenor character, without jeopardising his voice. In other words, he may use more chest than middle register, or more head than middle register. It is never dangerous for a singer to bring down his head register, but too much chest register in the middle range may sooner or later have bad consequences. Young baritones who intend to sing bass-baritone roles like Wotan, will easily endanger their high notes by mixing too much chest into their middle register, in their efforts to bring maturity into their voices.

The Viennese teacher and writer, Otto Iro,[1] makes an instructive comparison. He calls chest resonance 'earth' and head resonance 'water'. When earth is mixed with water, we get 'clay'. With more water the clay becomes thinner; with more earth the clay becomes thicker. In a dramatic or heroic role, the singer uses more 'earth', whilst in lyric phrases he uses more 'water'. Siegfried's forge song, for instance, needs more 'earth', Tamino more 'water'.

There are two kinds of failure in singing: one that makes us sing less well, but does no harm, and the other which endangers the voice itself. A tenor who sings Siegfried may mix too much head resonance into his middle range, if his voice is not powerful enough for the part: and it will not jeopardise his voice. But a singer who uses too much chest resonance and too little head resonance in his middle range, particularly in his transition notes,

[1] *Diagnostic der Stimme* (Diagnosis of the Voice), Vienna Verlag, Die Stimmbildung, 1923.

may overstrain his voice: a serious failing which may sooner or later be disastrous.

Here are a few examples of musical phrases which always need to be sung with the right mixture of head and chest resonance.

A bass who sings the following aria from the *Magic Flute* must start the very first note with sufficient head resonance:

When he sings Rossini's aria 'La Calummia' (*Il Barbiere di Siviglia*) he will start in chest voice, but the second part of the phrase is best sung with head-resonance mixed into the middle range.

The baritone singing Rigoletto's scene in the third act will start with a great deal of chest resonance, otherwise the phrase would lack the necessary deep feeling.

On the other hand, the more the same singer uses his head resonance the more easily will he sing Figaro's aria in Rossini's *Barbiere di Siviglia:*

Even the *tenore robusto* has to use head resonance from the very first notes of *Celeste Aida*, otherwise the F will not be sufficiently pure and floating:

But when the same tenor sings *Otello*, he needs a full-sounding, big voice based on reliable chest resonance from the first phrase:

though the beautiful *duo*, and especially the last two notes, have to be sung in good head resonance.[1]

The Chapter 'Chest Register' has several examples of typical chest passages for women's voices. A dramatic soprano appearing as Leonore (*Fidelio*) will only be able to master this difficult role if she has a biggish, dark and mature-sounding voice, especially in the middle range. The opening of the great arias recitative:

and the first phrases of the legato section have to be sung with the proper resonance, but not in chest voice.[2]

---

[1] I was fortunate enough to hear the famous first Otello, Francesco Tamagno, when he gave a concert with orchestra in Vienna. The audience did not want to leave until he had thundered out Otello's entrance phrase and the death scene. Unfortunately, I did not hear him sing his master-role on stage, but frequently heard Leo Slezak, who was undoubtedly one of the greatest Otellos.

[2] It has been explained how chest resonance can be checked by holding the hands against the upper part of the chest. A contralto, mezzo-soprano or dramatic soprano will feel a similar vibration in her middle range, but it will not be so strong as when she sings real chest-notes.

A soprano who sings Aida also needs a big dramatic voice, for throughout the whole part she has heavy dramatic singers as partners; she cannot be a really good Aida unless she has good head-notes and the ability to use her head-resonance in the middle and even the lowest range:

Even the low notes in this phrase have to be sung with much head resonance, otherwise it cannot be ended in a floating pianissimo, and there will be an audible break in the voice.

One of the most exquisite melodies Verdi ever wrote is the heavenly theme in the farewell *duo* (*Aida*, last act). Neither soprano nor tenor can hope to sing the phrase perfectly unless they are able to mix a great deal of head resonance into the transitional notes:

Another good example of where head resonance has to be mixed into the lower range is the following phrase from Aida's *Nile Aria*[1]:

It is essential to sing the first and second parts (as indicated)

[1] This advice about the Nile Aria has helped many singers who worked with me; naturally it is not a general rule.

with a great deal of head resonance, in a floating way, but with a rather darker colour. The transitional notes in particular have to be sung as if they belonged to the lower part of the phrase. The following ♪ has to be treated as a high note, but it should closely resemble the previous ♪ .

Sopranos without a particularly high range, in other words, those for whom high C is a limit, should keep the dark colour to ♪ . They may prepare the position of the high C by opening the mouth to an easy natural smile, but slowly and carefully, and not abruptly. The singer must feel exactly when and how to open, otherwise the high C will never be safe and beautiful. Just as in car driving, the instructor teaches how and when to turn the wheel so as to turn correctly, the teacher can only advise on precise timing and preparation of the position of the high note; the performer has to manoeuvre it. I always advise my students not to disturb the beautiful phrase by breaking it too often, but to sing it in one breath from (1) to (2), provided that the singer is not afraid of the high C. If this happens, there is a vicious circle. She will not be able to prepare the phrase correctly—her high C will not be as good as she hoped—so she will be afraid when she sings the phrase again.

A dramatic soprano has to have a good head register as well as a reliable middle and chest register; the more she is able to mix head resonance into the lower range, the better she will sing, and the longer the period of her best singing will last.

A coloratura soprano on the other hand must know how to sing certain phrases in full voice by mixing in some middle-range resonance (any idea of chest resonance would be erroneous in this connection). Unmixed head-notes are not enough if she wishes to sing such parts as Violetta (*Traviata*) and so on. Even if she sings Lucia with effective coloratura, all she will be able to offer will be a puppet without feeling, and not a romantic character. (cf. p. 115, 'Coloratura Singing'.)

In Lieder-singing, it is essential to mix head resonance with the middle and even the lowest range. It is quite inconceivable without complete mastery of head resonance. To mention only one example out of thousands, Schubert's *Ständchen* (Serenade):

The first note has to be sung with the same head resonance as the higher note, regardless of whether it is sung by a male or a female singer, by a tenor or a baritone.

Naturally, although the singer is fully aware of his registers and their best use, the audience should not notice any difficulty in the blending or tone. The teacher must make this quite clear.

To sum up: a singer who does not understand how registers function will sooner or later have trouble in equalising his low, middle and high notes; given other assets and a healthy voice, which he does not overstrain, he will probably manage to use his voice more or less successfully for a certain period: his ignorance can only harm his own voice. But a teacher who denies the existence of registers or does not understand their use can be a real danger, even though a gifted singer may always emerge from his school. There is always an exception to prove the rule. The legendary Viennese rogue, 'Der Liebe Augustin', fell dead-drunk into a ditch of plague-stricken corpses, slept himself sober, and walked off unharmed!

BREATH CONTROL AND HEAD RESONANCE
—GUARDIAN ANGELS OF THE VOICE—

A famous doctor once claimed that man's life-span depends on the state of his blood-vessels. Other doctors may well stress other factors, but agreement would be reached about fundamentals.

The practice and teaching of singing is not a science but an art, although it is based on technical principles, and universal agreement on essentials is asking the impossible.

Opinions on breathing differ more widely than on any other topic in singing, which itself is the most controversial branch of music study. But most performers and instructors will probably agree that breath-control and head resonance are essentials. The minority not only deny the importance of breath-control, but deprecate its training. The masters of the *bel canto* era, they say, did not explain *how* or *where* to take breath. They were merely concerned with how it had to be used once it had been taken. Tosi[1] for instance, only says that the singer must be taught to manage the breath so that he will always have enough. Caccini[2] writes: 'Per l'eccellenca di essa arte, ne e tanto necessaria la buona voce per essa quanto la respirazione del fiato, per volersene poi, ove fa più di mestiere . . .' Freely translated, this means 'Mastering the breath, like having a good voice, is essential to good singing. It must be used where it is most needed.' There are many other passages to the same effect.

Even in his excellent work about the *castrati* and their accomplishments, Franz Haböck says nothing to explain how these extraordinary singers, possessed of almost interminable breath, learnt or taught the art of breath control. All we get are ambiguous and generalised instructions. 'Take breath easily, not tightly: inhale quickly and noiselessly, let it out evenly, in a floating way, even in dramatic singing,' etc. But there is no sign of an exercise!

Even in modern times, a student may well be confused by the information given in authoritative books. Take a book called *Authentic Voice Production* by W. Warren Shaw, A.M., Lecturer at Pennsylvania University:

'Thoughts of breath control and breath support in the

[1] Piere Francesco Tosi (1647–1727), famous *castrato* and teacher, author of *Opinioni de' Cantori Antichi e Moderni* (1723).
[2] Guilio Caccini (1550–1618), singer, composer of *Nuove Musiche*.

minds of students who are trying to learn to use their voices properly are, all in all, about the most destructive thoughts that they could possibly entertain . . . to control the breath purposefully is scientifically untenable and practically subversive of desired ends.'

Compare this with the following, taken from *Resonance in Singing and Speaking* by Thomas Fillebrown, M.D., lecturer on voice development, copyright 1891:

'. . . enough has been said in the preceding chapter to make clear the necessity for breath control, and to show what constitutes this control for the singer—the professional breather.'

Opinions are even more conflicting if a student consults singing teachers. So far as breathing is concerned, they may be divided into five main groups:

1. Does not discuss it. If asked, may reply 'Breathe as you do in speaking, that is all.'

2. Believes in one of the many exaggerated methods. Fails to emphasise the importance of note-placement, and over-exercises on breathing, causing muscular tension.

3. Tells the student to 'take a big breath' with his upper chest, and disregards the grave defect of lifting the shoulders. (Mercifully this group is slowly disappearing!)

4. Tells the student to feel the lateral expansion of his ribs while inhaling. Others recommend feeling the expansion of the back muscles. (See 5.)

5. Stresses how breath-control functions, and the need it serves, *at the right time*. He shows how his own abdominal muscles function when he sings. By using them correctly, the lateral expansion of the lower ribs and back abdominal muscles *automatically* come into action, just as in a car the rear lights flash on when the driver stops.

One good explanation is the following: Breath is the raw material which the singer transforms into continuous, floating sound waves. The more raw material a factory has at its disposal, the bigger its output. In daily life we only inhale what we need to stay alive. At automatic intervals the city-dweller lifts his chest and fills the *upper* part of his lungs. If he goes out to the country or seaside, he takes a *deep* breath, just as he does for a doctor. In other words, during routine living we do not use all our breathing capacity, but in singing we need all the breath (or raw material) we have got. Some singers, of course, use less breath than others. A Wagnerian singer naturally uses more than a light coloratura soprano. Others use less because they do not tense their throat and neck muscles. When there are no hindrances in neck and throat, the whole stock of breath can be transformed into notes. Exercises can be given to relax the muscles, so that this can take place. It is like an engineer who diverts a mountain-stream into a canal, so that the whole volume of water runs freely. Those who insist on breathing as in ordinary life are like engineers who disregard the possibilities of hydraulic power!

We can also think of breath-control as being like the management of money. We acquire as much as we can and use it as well as possible. Some people never have enough because they spend their whole income, whilst others carefully balance up spending against income.

There are eight main principles in breathing for singing:

1. The quantity has to be increased by using the abdominal cavities, which are generally neglected in daily life.

2. The outgoing breath has to be controlled by the abdominal muscles, so that it will be adequate for any note or phrase.

3. All the available breath must be transformed into tone. (Caruso was a past-master at this.)

4. An emergency reserve must be allowed for, just as in driving

it is unwise to use the last drop of petrol! Otherwise the voice may be overstrained.

5. The chest should never be moved, either in inhalation or exhalation. By standing erect before and during inhalation, the chest cavities can receive no more air; it then goes to the abdominal cavities, which supply the breath used in singing. By constant inward pressure on the abdominal wall (or exhalation) all the air there can be used without using the breath in the chest cavities.

6. The abdominal cavities should not be filled to capacity, otherwise a phrase cannot be attacked well, with smooth, clear tone.

7. The breath must be prepared by a moment of suspension. (See p. 79.)

8. Regular exercises must be practised, and the teacher must check constantly that they are being done correctly, so that they can become quite automatic. (See p. 82.)

Abdominal Breathing

We PRESS on the muscles of the abdomen continually, but do not PUSH them. I ask a girl to hiccup and check on what muscles she is using. They are just the same as those used in elimination and breathing. Daily exercises before breakfast will strengthen these muscles. Caruso liked to show friends and visitors how strong his were by moving the grand piano with them ! But avoid exaggeration, which causes tension.

Abdominal Breathing[1] has numerous advantages:

(a) It is easier to sing a smooth phrase when the air comes

[1] I know that many good singers have a different method of breathing, but I have always been in good company by using my breath in the way described. Battistini breathed this way, as did my own teacher, Alexander Haydter (bass-baritone at the Vienna Court Opera under Gustav Mahler), having learnt it from Francesco d'Andrade (1859–1921). D'Andrade in turn learnt it from Miraglia and Giorgio Roncone (1810–1890). It was also used by my teacher in Lieder-singing, Franz Steiner, a student and successor of Johannes Meschaert and his teacher Julius Stockhausen, the first great Lieder-singer, who was a pupil of Manuel Garcia.

from a greater distance, i.e. from the diaphragm, and not the short way from the chest. Chest breathing is always dangerous as we inhale *too* much *too* quickly, and so press on neck and throat muscles.

(b) It reduces the possibility of strain in the throat, which leads to throaty singing. If we have to lift something heavy, we prepare by tautening the right muscles, so as not to overwork hand and arm muscles. If the abdominal muscles are not reinforced before a big top note, the throat muscles automatically come into action. The breath that is taken before dramatic notes and phrases must be in direct relation to what is going to be sung. A singer has to learn to co-ordinate throat and abdominal muscles rather as a driver has to keep his hands on the wheel, and his feet ready to use the pedals.

(c) Notes and phrases sung with abdominal breathing sound much more expressive. It is easy to understand why. By using these muscles, we influence the sympathetic nervous system. We feel all our emotions in the abdomen, so that when we are upset we cannot eat or keep down our food. When we laugh we 'hold our belly'. Michelangelo was right to represent Moses' emotion (in the famous statue) by having him hold his stomach with his right hand.

Caruso frequently, while on tours through Europe, liked to visit synagogues on his free evenings to listen to the cantors, who have a tradition of warmly persuasive devotional singing, ergo, with the proper use of their abdominal muscles.

Faking Emotions Causes Strain

Under emotional stress, people tend to lift their shoulders and chest. An actor or singer may try to incorporate these character-

istics in the parts he plays. This faked emotional state may become
an integral part of his technique, and can be very strenuous and
fatiguing. Inexperienced singers should be careful not to substitute
faked emotions of voice or body instead of genuine mastery,
particularly in parts like Santuzza, Canio, Butterfly, José, Carmen,
etc.

Preparation of Breath

Ordinary breathing can take place in two counts, breathing-in
and breathing-out. Breathing for singing needs three: (1) inhale,
(2) hold the breath, (3) exhale (and sing). In legato there is
absolutely no need to rush at a breath, and this moment of
suspension is essential for good singing:

I	II	III
TAKE A BREATH	WAIT A MOMENT	SING

(as before jumping into the water)

and not:

I	II
TAKE A BREATH	SING!

It is easy to understand this. If we throw a ball or fire a shot,
we are more likely to hit the target if we have a moment to prepare, and we also gain more strength. *Snatched breaths* are
necessary in quick phrases, where even experienced singers sometimes find it difficult to be in a ready position. Generally speaking,
the more difficult the note, the more careful must be the preparation. *Test for wasting breath.* The Italian masters recommended the
following exercise if they suspected breath was being wasted:
they held a mirror or a lighted candle close to the student's
mouth while he was singing. A singer who does not waste breath
sings without clouding the mirror or putting out the candle!

Where to Take Breath

Where to take breath is generally decided by the musical phrase, though sometimes it is the words. It is the note or word *after* the breathing-space which matters most. Avoid making a pause before an unimportant word. A good speaker knows that nothing can emphasise a word or sentence so much as a pause—a 'pause for effect'.

For various reasons, a singer may be short of breath before he finishes a legato phrase, so that the last note lacks lustre. An expert singer will start the next note with exactly the same colour, tone quality and volume, but will develop the notes within the phrase. A less expert singer will start with a big note, and so break up the continuity of the phrase. A good singer never lets his audience know how much he has drawn on his breath-reserve.

The pause for breath in legato-singing must be as well managed as a violinist's change of bow, so that it is hardly noticeable. An expert singer always takes breath in good time, and not from sheer necessity, just as an adult eats when he has a break. A baby on the other hand will cry for food as soon as he feels hungry. A singer breathes after his last note rather than before the next one, just as a typist will automatically space *after* her last word instead of *before* the one that follows. This is a very important point: it is like a boxer who returns at once to the defensive after a flurry of attack. In legato it is quite wrong to relax, and then take a breath in a hurry.

Breath-Taking in Arias—How the Composer can Help

Sometimes the composer allows the singer time to take breath: Richard Wagner, whose dramatic talents were not inferior to his musical genius, seldom left a singer in doubt. Here is Telramund's first utterance:

LOHENGRIN, Act I, Scene I

DANK, KÖ-NIG, DIR, DASS DU ZU RICH-TEN KAMST DIE WAHRHEIT KÜND'ICH, UN-TREU, IST MIR GREMD

Beethoven seldom wrote comfortably for the voice, and in Florestan's aria in *Fidelio* found the right expression for the prisoner's ecstasy by forcing the singer into a very high range. The pauses were probably meant to characterise Florestan's excitement rather than give the singer time to breathe, but the chance is there:

At other times the singer has to work it out for himself. In Radames' famous aria *Celeste Aida*, for instance Verdi wrote in few pauses; the singer has to make time by shortening the last note before the pause:

In the Countess' second aria (*Dove sono*) in *Le Nozze di Figaro*, the singer gains time to breathe by a moment of graceful suspension:

A

AH

O and U

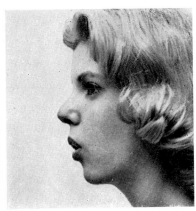
Correct O(U)

Exercises for mouth position

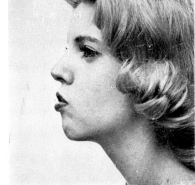
Wrong O(U)

Exercises for breathing correctly

Tiredness Shows in Lack of Abdominal Support

Physical tiredness often afflicts a singer towards the end of a performance. He may have been singing against a large orchestra, or rushing about the stage, as Siegfried does. He may lack the energy to reinforce his abdominal muscles before singing a high note. It will then sound throaty by comparison with the high notes of the first act. Sooner or later, this could lead to loss of voice.

Battistini's Last Concert in Vienna

I remember Battistini's last concert in Vienna—the penultimate of his life. He was nearly seventy at the time. Although as usual the first half of his programme consisted of taxing arias and songs, he only left the stage once during the whole evening to rest in his dressing-room. The rest of the time, he waited in the wings without sitting down. I was privileged to visit him after the concert, and asked him why he had not sat down. He whispered in my ear 'Sono vecchio' (I am old). He had conserved his strength by cutting out any relaxation which could have dissipated his energies; he knew that perfect singing requires the support of the whole body. In dramatic arias, his mighty body stood like a statue. As few great artists, he knew the secrets of real bel canto, and for nearly half a century was able to sing in public with perfect technique. In his art he exemplified the basic rule that the more economically the breath is used, the greater the intensity and beauty of tone, and the longer the voice will last.

Breathing Exercise

Practise this in the morning before getting dressed, if possible at the same time each day. Make it a part of your morning routine, like brushing your teeth. In good weather do it before an open window.

1. *Stand erect,* not stiffly, with the chest held high. (The old Italian masters used to say 'come una statua' (like a statue).)

2. *Inhale slowly* through a half-opened mouth, and at the same time lift the arms upwards above your head. Count 1-2-3.

3. *Hold the breath* for a moment (as in underwater swimming) with the arms above the head.

4. *Exhale slowly,* while the arms circle slowly round to position (1).

Repeat this ten times a day, later increasing the number systematically. Other breathing exercises may be added, but do not do less than 10 daily, or more than 10 twice a day.

Exercises to Strengthen Abdominal Muscles

1. Stretch arms forward at eye-level as for diving, swing them from one side to the other, spinning round from waist without moving the feet.

2. Stretch your arms above your head, bend down as far as possible without bending the knees.

3. Stretch the arms above the head and turn from right to left, i.e. when you turn right, you lift the left arm and vice versa. Arms must be straight.

4. Keep erect, arms at your sides. Bend your knees slowly, keeping the heels together. The knees can splay out.

5. Stand on tip-toe and bounce up and down in quick rhythm, holding the arms sideways.

HIGH NOTES

Young singers and, alas, some teachers, try to reach top notes the 'dramatic way', i.e. by singing them in dramatic arias and songs. This is dangerous even for mature dramatic voices, but for lyric voices it usually spells destruction. It is widely believed that the higher a singer can sing, the more success he will have. Young students like to discover whether they can reach top notes and top C becomes a goal amongst students as it is famous amongst laymen.

There are two possibilities: to have high notes by nature, or to develop them later. They can be developed either by forcing or by systematic work with a good teacher. Until they are automatic, a student concentrates on them too much. 'Isn't that how it should be?' asks the layman. No, the singer should never think of the note itself, but only of how to prepare for it.[1] An untrained diver jumping off a board will always think of the moment when he hits the water. The experienced diver concentrates on preparing for the dive, knowing that if he jumps properly, the dive will turn out well. If a singer has not been systematically trained, he will be unsure and nervous when he sees a high note coming.

High notes, one could say, call forth two types of singer. *One looks forward to them with pleasure, knowing them to be sure effects, and the audience looks forward with him. The other type is afraid, and his fear affects his audience and his singing.*

What can be done with a pupil who is afraid of a high note? He must be given confidence. The longer high notes have been forced, and the more fear there is, the more difficult will be the correction of this great handicap. It is no good expecting a miracle, although the results achieved by a good teacher sometimes seem like miracles. Every student constitutes a separate problem, and before beginning to cure a 'high-note' phobia a teacher must be quite sure of the reason the singer finds them difficult, and the exact limits of his voice.

Jean de Reszke advised tenors to use the vowel *ü* on high notes, but for some singers this would be fatal as the throat has to be free and relaxed. Used by good tenors, *ü* gives roundness to high

---

[1] Caruso once mentioned in an interview in Berlin that the note before the high note is the most important.

notes, but it could easily become an obstacle by pressing on the muscles of neck and throat. High notes or a better high range can only be acquired by gaining head resonance (q.v.) which will give brilliance and greater facility: phrases in a high range will also come much more easily. The first aim is to sing them easily: brilliance and volume will follow. If a nail is hammered into a wall, it is better to start with a thin one. If the wall offers no resistance, a thicker one can safely be used, otherwise there may be an ugly hole.

It is always risky to sing high notes as big notes straight away. Results are naturally better when high notes have not been previously forced. When a teacher is developing high notes, he must always match up the newly-acquired notes to the middle and lower range of the voice (see Legato, Registers, etc.). The best test for this essential blending is to sing a phrase in the lower range and immediately another very high phrase. For instance: aria Leonora, *Il Trovatore,* act 4:

A well-blended voice should never show any difference in place-ment and sound when the phrase is repeated in the middle range after the high phrase. Old-time-singers like Battistini always repeated each aria: they sang the smooth legato in the middle range exactly in the same manner and sound when they sang it for the second time.

Gestures should not be used to indicate where placement should be felt (see 'General Approach'). Right placement should be brought about by exercises, and the student can then try and explain where he feels the placement, which should tally with the teacher's experience. This works much better than a theoretical description, which tends to be misleading. Mature artists often describe their own sensations, but cannot be sure that the student feels the same (see Lilly Lehmann, 'Vowels & Consonants', footnote, p. 54).

It is well-nigh impossible to recommend exercises for high notes, but these are important principles to remember:

1. High notes have different placements and sensations from middle-range placement, and require special exercises to develop them. (See 'Resonance in Singing and Speaking.')

2. High notes generally need more breath support than lower notes. A high coloratura soprano or light tenor may disregard this rule, but neither will be able to sing ringing top notes. A higher note in *forte* needs more preparation and more breath support. When a driver wants to climb a steep hill, he has to change gear and use more petrol, or the car will come to a halt.

3. A singer should not sing a high note in public unless he has sung a whole tone higher in exercises. In other words he should always have a reserve. Whatever he sings, he should feel

(*a*) He can sing higher;
(*b*) He can sing louder;
(*c*) He can hold the note longer.

Manuel Garcia II liked to repeat his father's advice:
'Never let another person see the bottom of your purse.'
I have always preferred to work with pupils who have never tried to sing high notes at all. It is then much easier to increase their range.

If a beginner can sing good and effortless top notes, he should know *why* they are good. Many singers, including men and women of great names and reputations, have asked me why they could no longer reach their top notes easily, 'and my top notes' they will say, 'were always my strong point'. I suspect it is because their teachers never explained why they were good in the first place. It is not enough to do something well; one must also know why.

The fact that audiences are always impressed by brilliant high notes leads some singers to exaggerate by singing too many, or by singing them tastelessly. Thanks to the growing authority of conductors, interpolating high notes seems to be going out of fashion, but many coloratura sopranos still offend in this direction: a hard interpolated head note in *forte* often goes to show that the soprano cannot sing a full *forte* note on the G and A flat below.

Some time ago, a sensational press report appeared about a London teacher who had discovered a young girl with an even wider range than that of Yma Sumac. Such sensations belong to the collection of rarities of the late Phineas T. Barnum, which included the calf with two heads. Singing is an art and not a sport, and curiosities of this kind have nothing to do with music. *A singer is good because he sings well, not because he can sing higher than another.*

THE MIDDLE REGISTER—HOME OF THE VOICE

Whatever the voice, the middle register is the most important, because it is the one that is used most, whether in speaking or singing. Even in arias and songs with a high range, the middle register provides the foundation. When the middle register is easy and a singer can pass smoothly to both higher and lower notes, he is in good vocal health. I call the middle register a *home* because it is like a parental home, where a person can always find help and understanding, whatever the storms of life. Those without even a temporary refuge are likely to go astray or get lost. A singer with a well-placed middle register will not come to so much harm even if he forces his top notes—but like a home it is not a gift to be abused. The middle register can be injured if the high register is wrongly used. It is the first to show signs of strain (e.g. hoarseness, q.v.) and such warnings should be acted upon as quickly as possible.

Patti corroborates the importance of the middle register in an interesting interview she once gave (as she sang in public for forty-seven years, her evidence has much weight):

'People who cultivate the voice have widely different ideas on what constitutes the best methods of its preservation. If I gave lessons I should cultivate the middle notes, and the voice of the singer would be good at the age of a hundred. The whole harm to a voice comes in pushing it up and down, in trying to add notes to its compass.

' "How high can you sing?" seems to be the operative question. But what about the foundation part of the voice, the middle notes? My success is founded on those notes, and there can be no enduring success without them. How many can sing very high and yet cannot sing *Home, Sweet Home*! Some pooh-pooh the idea of the difficulty in that simple melody. But it is more difficult to sing *Home, Sweet Home* than the waltz song from *Romeo and Juliet*, because of its demands upon the development of the voice. Without the beautiful middle notes there is no cantabile, and upon the proper development of these, and the avoidance of strain by forcing high and low notes, the enduring powers of the singer depend.

'High gymnastics are very beautiful; but, lose the middle notes, and you lose all. The very high and the very low notes are the ornaments, but what good are Gobelins and pictures if you have no house to hang them in?'

The middle register is much more vulnerable in women than in men. Even at the peak of her career, Jenny Lind's voice showed signs of 'veiling' in the middle register. Although it is difficult to discuss voices of the past, her case is most instructive. At ten she was made an *aktriselev* (scholar) at the Royal Theatre in her native Stockholm. She had singing lessons at this early age as well as tuition in dancing and acting. At eighteen she enjoyed great triumphs in such taxing parts as Agathe in *Freischütz*, though some press critics warned her that she was 'overstepping the limits which Nature had set for her'. She was singing roles such as Donna Anna in *Don Giovanni*, Armida (Gluck), Julia (*La Vestale*) and even Bellini's *Norma*. Fortunately she realized that she lacked a solid technique. She decided to study in Paris for a year with Manuel Garcia II, and undertook a strenuous concert tour in the provinces to collect the necessary funds, which greatly endangered her voice. By then she was Sweden's most famous singer, with the title of 'Royal Singer'. She was understandably piqued when she sang for the maestro and he told her 'Mademoiselle vous n'avez plus de voix' (You have no voice left). But she followed his advice, and rested her voice completely. She went off to the country, stopped singing entirely and talked very little. Then she began her lessons. She has related how ignorant she was about breathing, blending the registers, and other technical processes. After a year's meticulous study, she once more appeared as Norma at the Stockholm Opera, and enjoyed an extraordinary success.

The help which an outstanding teacher can give an exceptional pupil was never more fully recognised than on this occasion. The King gave Garcia a high order and Sweden's most famous university bestowed an Honorary Doctorate on him. Jenny Lind went on to conquer the world—her name is still a household word. The 'veiling' of her middle range was clearly the result of over-working a delicate voice, insufficiently trained, at too early an age. But few singers can find a complete panacea in the medicine-chest of a great singing-master!

Lyric sopranos and high lyric tenors must never overwork the middle register, which for them is very delicate. Coloratura sopranos too often have a weak and childish middle register. W. J. Henderson described the inexpressive notes of some coloraturas as 'baby-talk' when he was commenting on Luisa Tetrazzini's Violetta at the Metropolitan (Jan. 16, 1908), and it is a good description of what is still a vogue amongst coloraturas. It may be related to the hard, forced head-notes in forte discussed elsewhere (coloratura and agility, p. 115) for both 'baby-talk' and hard head-notes lack the undertone of emotion which is needed to move an audience. 'White' tone in the middle range is not at all dangerous: on the contrary, the singer who uses it will never jeopardise her top range, and will find clean runs and acrobatics very simple. But this facility offers sensations of relatively short duration, like fireworks, which can stimulate but not move. Pyrotechnics cannot express the character or fate of a heroine such as Lucia di Lammermoor: but how they can thrill an audience.

Jean de Reszke often pointed out that *expressiveness in singing comes from the middle register and the bridge notes to the high register*.[1] All male voices, dramatic sopranos, mezzos and contraltos need their middle register to show emotion. At the same time it is essential to remember the cardinal law which holds for all voices, both male and female:

NEVER FORCE THE MIDDLE RANGE, never try to give it more maturity and importance than it has by nature.

CHEST NOTES IN WOMEN
FALSETTO IN MEN

An old politician once interrupted a passionate argument between two colleagues by saying 'Two people can fight if one says WHITE and the other says BLACK. But if one says

---

[1] 'A brilliant or vocally perfect high note is the result of innate or acquired skill, and makes its own effect. Hence a singer should show emotion in lower notes, and particularly in transitional notes.'

WHITE and the other says APPLE-PIE, fighting is ridiculous'.

Singing has many such arguments. Teachers and performers have long been confused by differences of opinion even amongst unimpeachable authorities, who often used terms quite differently from each other. Both Manuel Garcia II and Julius Stockhausen, not to mention others, describe the middle register in women's voices as *falsetto*, which for most people means a register in men's voices. Just imagine what would happen if an important blood vessel had different names according to the school of medicine that was describing it![1]

In this chapter I shall attempt to define two specific terms over which there is much confusion.

The Chest Register in Women's Voices

There is always confusion of terminology here, because *chest notes* and *chest registers* are commonly used in contradistinction to *head notes* and *head register* in both men's and women's voices, whereas the female chest register has its own special quality. The low notes of men do not sound as a separate register, and the transition to and from the middle register can be made quite smoothly and imperceptibly.   Women have an audible break between the two registers (see 'Registers of the Voice'). In

women it comprises the notes between and

contraltos sometimes have to sing

---

[1] At the 3rd Congress of the International Society for Logopaedia and Phoniatry in Vienna in 1920, I was one of the invited lecturers and heard the late Professor Hugo Stern give an excellent talk on 'The need for a generally acknowledged nomenclature for the physiology, pathology and training of the voice'. Unfortunately it was impossible to please all the members of the Society and the fine plans were abandoned.

Dramatic sopranos, mezzo-sopranos and contraltos all require it, and it is essential for opera-singing and for singing with orchestra. Many make the mistake of using it all the time, which is most unwise, as in some phrases chest notes are quite out of place. Generally speaking, as well as being indispensable, a well-functioning chest register is a sign of a healthy, well-trained voice. But it must not be over-robust. Female chest notes have great power, but exaggeration is ugly and dangerous, as Bernard Shaw frequently pointed out in his music criticism.

Some teachers advise against singing in chest

register (Italian singers will even take chest

register). What is certain is that *abuse of the upper limit* will sooner or later cause trouble. 'Trouble' means a much more striking break between chest notes and the adjacent notes sung in the middle register. It can be made somewhat less audible by 'colouring' (see 'Registers'), i.e. by mixing head register into the chest and middle notes. Sometimes, when listening to an unknown opera on records or radio, one singer sounds like two, contralto and soprano, because she sings higher than F in the chest register, and the gap is too big to be bridged by colouring.

Singers exceed the natural limit because of the relative weakness of the adjacent notes. As has frequently been stressed, young girls seldom have the notes characteristic of older women, though there are exceptions among genuine contraltos and mezzo-sopranos.

Chest notes have to be sung in an easy, natural way. Many teachers are utterly against the use of chest notes, often because they have never used them themselves in singing (light sopranos

or coloraturas do not need them), or because as male teachers
they have never had to teach them to women. Manuel Garcia II
had a unique way of teaching them. He would ask a girl to
imitate the quacking of a duck: the astonished girl would try and
oblige, and Garcia would then encourage her to hold these
unnatural sounds as if they were notes in normal singing. It
often helped the student to find the way to produce them. Nowadays, of course, a teacher merely has to ask a student to imitate
any female 'pop' singer, whose technique is generally based on
an exaggerated use of the chest register. The conscious or unconscious imitation of the 'sexy' style of robust negro women
singers is a most disastrous vogue amongst young girls (see 'Pop'
singing). To my mind it is a sign of decadence in musical taste
to be pleased by a pretty blonde who sings with a man's voice.
As the old French proverb says 'never trust a woman with a
man's voice!' The raucous, masculine chest register of such

singers extends from  to

then there comes a thin voice which sounds extremely weak and
quite different.

Chest-notes have to be used tastefully, or the whole musical
line is disturbed. In the following example:

an audible break has to be avoided, and only skilled colouring
can overcome the difficulty. Although the low phrases in this
aria are not sung forte, the chest register is needed to give the
right tone-colour and expression. The whole of the following

phrase of Amneris was clearly intended to be sung in chest voice, since it has to be sung with great energy while the orchestra plays *ben marcato*. It could not be heard unless the chest register was used:

It is the upper limit for chest notes, and difficult to avoid singing G in the chest register. Some contraltos manage to sing the first part with dark-coloured middle notes and only *le furie ho in cor* in chest.

The following very characteristic song for low woman's voice should not be sung unless it can be sung in the chest register:

This aria:

has to be sung with deep emotion. The singer has to have a full middle register, and the low notes need singing in chest register, but without any difference of colour.

If a singer is doubtful whether to sing a note or phrase in chest or in middle register, it is better to choose the latter. In any case, it is always better not to sing a low note at the outset of a middle-range phrase as a chest-note. Even when two or three could be sung in chest, as in Brahms's *Mainacht*:

They should be given the same dark colouring as the rest. *Even the lowest notes need mixing with head resonance.* (See 'Registers', p. 72, Lieder-singing.) A good singer should be able to sing the lowest notes mezza voce and even piano, always most effective.

The chest register of some well-trained contraltos and mezzos sometimes sounds like a tenor singing an octave above. This seldom lasts long enough to be a real disturbance. Richard Wagner quickly gained remarkable mastery of the chest register through working as an opera conductor. In the first act of *Lohengrin*, at the chorus entry after Lohengrin's arrival, there is an effect which is unique in operatic literature. The magical sound of the mixed chorus is obtained in a very simple way: the melody is sung by the contraltos at the bottom of their range and by the tenors one octave higher, mezza-voce, in falsetto:

This unusual sound combination[1] expresses the feeling of this scene in a wonderful way, and brings me to the second part of my chapter.

[1] Otto Nicolai (1810–1849), composer of the *Merry Wives of Windsor*, wrote in 1837 that the contralto chorus parts in the Sistine Chapel were not sung by *castrati*, like the soprano parts, but by *falsetti*.

Falsetto

This word is often misunderstood. It is a register in men's voices, and occurs when a male singer tries to sing soft notes above his natural range. Why great teachers such as Manuel Garcia, Stockhausen, etc., used *falsetto* for the middle register of women's voices may never be guessed.

Falsetto implies something which is false, not true, not natural. The best description is to be found in Webster's Dictionary: 'A false or artificial voice. That voice of a man which lies above his natural voice.' It was probably first applied to singers in liturgical music in the Roman Church, which does not admit the use of female singers. The soprano parts are normally sung by boys. But in the Sixteenth Century, the polyphonic *a cappella* style had reached such complexity that it was difficult for boys to master it during the relatively short period at their disposal (from eight to thirteen, about five years). Tenors took over the highest parts, which they could only do in an unnatural way, by singing *falsetto*. They were called *tenori falsetti* or simply *falsetti*. Later they were replaced by *castrati,* i.e. singers whose voices did not break, the result of a surgical operation.[1]

German vocal nomenclature uses the term *fisteln*, which is the same as *falsetto* except that it expects a cruder effect. Even when used with great finesse, *falsetto* singing is always unnatural. In normal singing the vocal cords vibrate as a whole, whilst in falsetto only the edges vibrate. The fact that falsetto notes sound like the notes of a woman or a boy has made some teachers conclude that it is a relic of pre-puberty. This belongs to the field of

[1] So long as the church required the musical services of such singers, the matter was glossed over, and the Church allegedly did not know how many boys were disfigured. Poor and greedy parents were seduced by the wealth that famous *castrati* could amass. All *castrati* came from Italy, and were connected with the Church. Even as early as 1562, a castrato called Hydronimus Rossinus was a member of the Papal Orchestra. They took important parts in operatic performances. The last-known castrato, Moreschi, made several recordings at the beginning of this century. (See 'Bel Canto' chapter.)

laryngology. A student should not bother too much about the theoretical side, but concentrate on the essentials:

1. Falsetto only exists in men's voices, and should never be used in reference to women's voices.

2. It uses an entirely different mechanism from normal production. The same note cannot be sung with two different mechanisms, in other words, *a falsetto note can never be developed to a chest or head note: nor can it be developed to a forte.*

3. A head note on the other hand can be sung by singers of both sexes. It is sung with partial or complete vibration of the skull and its cavities.

A piano (or pianissimo) note that can be developed to forte is a typical head-note and not a falsetto (see Voix Mixte, p. 98). Italian and 'Irish' lyric tenors sometimes get sensational effects (e.g. at the end of *Una furtiva lagrima,* in *l'Elisir d'Amore*) by singing a *decrescendo* from a head-note in *mezza voce* to a *fil di voce* which even a well-trained ear can take for falsetto except at very close range. In fact he is using the same technique as his female colleagues who possess good head resonance. Skilled singers minimise the break between pianissimo head-tone and falsetto by colouring the notes before and after the falsetto notes. Leo Slezak and Richard Tauber were past-masters of this art, though Caruso hardly ever sang in falsetto (he made a notable exception in Assad's song, Goldmark's *Queen of Sheba,* which can be heard on record).

The best way to discover whether a man can sing falsetto is to try him on *piano* notes, without forcing, above his normal range.

Composers use it repeatedly for special effects. As falsetto makes a man sound like a woman, Verdi asks for it when Falstaff imitates Mrs. Ford (*Falstaff*, Act I), and writes it so high that no baritone could reach it in a normal voice:

Puccini uses the same trick in *Boheme*, Act IV, where the baritone Marcello jokingly imitates a woman's singing and dancing:

Doctor Bartolo imitates Rosina in *Barbiere di Siviglia* by singing falsetto.

Wagner uses *Fistelstimme* instead of *falsetto* to describe the comical effect he wants from Mime in *Ring des Nibelungen*; he has to sound like a very old man with a childish voice. The same word is used to describe Beckmesser's comical sound in *Meistersinger*. A falsetto or fistula will sound like a woman's voice if it is reinforced, lose sweetness and end up by sounding like a yodel.

Yodelling, which does not belong to art-singing, is the capacity to alternate chest and falsetto notes in rapid succession. Women too can yodel if strong chest notes are alternated with thin middle or head notes.

Basses and baritones sing falsetto notes in songs when the head register is not reliable. They normally use it in opera for comic effects (as above), while tenors use it in serious arias and duets, and sometimes for sensational top notes.

7.

Voix Mixte

Voix mixte is another term which is often misunderstood, although much used by connoisseurs. To a teacher it indicates volume, and is used for *piano* or *mezza voce*, i.e. notes sung with half volume. It is confusing, because apart from so-called 'pure' head notes, every note is a 'mixed' note. But by a strange paradox the 'pure' head note will be the one described as *voix mixte*, i.e. sung *piano* or *mezza voce*!

The audience may well dissolve in ecstasy, but what really matters to a teacher is whether it is a *mezza voce* that can develop, and not a mere *falsetto*. The answer is fundamental to the art of singing, and it is sometimes extremely difficult to tell. Both can sound beautiful. An experienced teacher will not be deceived by the beauty of a note, anymore than a doctor is misled by the healthy appearance of a sick man.

Two Examples of Remarkable Development of Tenor Voices

Two famous tenors of the golden age of French opera, Gilbert Duprez and Hippolyte Roger, relate in their autobiographies that their voices were originally small. Duprez made his debut as Almaviva in *Barbiere*, and one critic wrote that it was necessary to sit in the prompt box to hear him! He later became a sensational dramatic tenor, singing such strenuous parts as Raoul (*Les Huguenots*) and Arnoldo (*Guglielmo Tell*).[1] Roger sang lyric and buffo tenor parts for ten years at the Opera Comique before singing at the Grand Opera, creating the immense dramatic role of Johann van Leyden (Meyerbeer's *Le Prophet*). It would be false to imagine that all voices could be so developed, if trained with sufficient energy. Only an experienced gardener knows whether a little flower will grow. It takes a wise teacher to be

---

[1] Donizetti wrote the part of Edgardo in *Lucia* for him, and incorporated his suggestion of having the dying hero imitate short phrases of the D major melody played by the cello in the last scene.

sure that a particular note can develop greater strength without sacrificing its quality.

LOW NOTES

A well-built and well-used voice generally has good low notes, for it will always show in this range if the top or middle range is forced.

Low notes never sound any louder when a singer tries to increase their volume by force. Forced high notes lose in quality, but can be made to sound louder, whereas forcing low notes often achieves the opposite effect; the note loses in quantity as well as in quality.

As explained in chapter 3 (Chest Notes in Women), the low notes of men do not sound like a separate register, whereas in women they form the chest register.

A high tenor will often lose in colour and volume the lower he sings. Low notes are never very important in light tenor arias and roles, and high tenors are seldom encouraged to force this range. Richard Wagner created a type of tenor whose range is more that of a baritone than a tenor. In fact the first Wagnerian tenors were often baritones who sang these tenor parts without special vocal training. Siegmund in *Die Walküre* calls for a very expressive middle range and good low notes. The typical Wagnerian baritone (Wotan, Hans Sachs, etc.) needs much lower notes than the baritone parts in other operas. Wagner later described his typical baritones as 'high bass' in contradistinction to low bass parts such as Fafner, Hunding and Hagen. They are really bass-baritones. The low notes of a real bass are as important as the high notes of a tenor; Mozart wrote the wonderful part of Sarastro in the *Magic Flute* for this type of singer. Good basses for these parts are even scarcer nowadays than high tenors, though they are not so rare in Russia as they are in Italy.

There is also another way of singing low notes, used by *basso*

RAMAKER LIBRARY

Northwestern College

Orange City, Iowa

buffos. Germans have an expression for this kind of low note. They call it *Strohbass*, in contrast to 'noble' low notes. Strohbass notes are often louder than normal notes, but they are mostly enlarged by forcing, and never sound beautiful.

Low notes lose in sonority and volume after strenuous singing and after a heavy cold.[1] Not even the best technique can help in such cases, for the more they are forced, the more they will lose in sound. The remedy is complete rest, just as for the middle register. If low notes consistently lose sonority, it is a stern warning that something is wrong. They should sound the same both before and after a performance.

[1] On the other hand some persons (singers) speak in a lower range when they have a cold and in the morning.

CHAPTER 4

TEACHING SKILL AND ITS USE

> 'The foundation of *bel canto* is the
> ability to sing legato. The founda-
> tion of *all* singing is the legato. It
> is just as essential to the delivery of
> Siegfried's Forge Song as it is to
> that of *Salut demeure* in *Faust.*'
>
> Footnote from *The Art of Singing,*
> by W. J. Henderson,
> Dial Press, New York, 1938.

LEGATO

By legato is meant the smooth linking of two or more notes. To
be linked without friction, two notes must be similar in sound and
produced in the same way. Legato singing is easier when the
notes belong to the same register. But with the help of head
resonance singers are able to link notes belonging to two completely different registers (see 'Register of the Voice'). They mix
the substance and colour of the two registers, just as two metals
are fused in the process of melting. When the singer of Carmen
comes to the phrase:

the first note needs mixing with head resonance, so that the F
sharp can be reached easily, without pushing or forcing.

When a tenor sings the aria *M'apparì* from Flotow's *Marta*,
he must use the right mixture from the first note, otherwise the
phrase will be uneven:

If he uses the same colour and mixture of registers for

he will be able to sing a smooth legato phrase, and sing it in a
single breath. Good legato facilitates longer phrases, because there
are no obstacles to be overcome, such as notes which do not
match. The first note has to go on sounding until it is released by
the next one. This must be done with the speed of lightning,
without interrupting the stream of breath. At the same time the
sound of a note has to be controlled before going on to the next.

How and When to Learn Legato

Training in legato is like barre-work in ballet, where the movements have to be as smooth, slow and continuous as possible. A
teacher who lacks the necessary ear and patience for legato will
never be able to build a voice properly. He should lay the corner-
stone in the first lessons without bothering with too much
explanation. As soon as a student has the rudiments of note-
placement, he needs exercises which link two and later more
notes within a small compass. There should be no words to
pronounce, and the intervals should be small. Simple songs and

arias should not be sung until legato is learnt. Those with big voices who want to sing dramatically find it much harder to master than small, sweet voices.

Lilly Lehmann sang from sixteen to seventy with a perfect legato style, and recommends the 'big scale' as a daily exercise for every professional singer[1] (*Meine Gesangskunst* (How to Sing), Verlag der Zukunft, Berlin, 1909). It is difficult to do well: I heard a similar exercise executed by Alessandro Bonci. Students with less than four years' intensive study behind them usually find it beyond them :

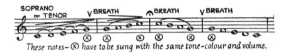

These notes— ⊗ have to be sung with the same tone-colour and volume.

Baritones, mezzo-sopranos and contraltos start a major third lower. Its highest note is decided by needing to be sung in *mezza voce*, and no note must be forced.

The following exercise can be very helpful for less advanced students:

The top note must *never* be pushed

hold the note F a moment, and start moving the lower jaw slowly and continuously, so that the top note (now G) is sung

[1] See 'Messa di Voce', p. 114.

while the jaw is in motion. Go on moving it until the starting note is reached again. *As a preparatory exercise,* take a mirror and in a smiling mouth-position move the lower jaw downward slowly and continuously, the slower the better. This exercise cannot harm a student even if it is sung at home several times a day. He will realize how useful it is when he begins to sing it with his teacher. It is also an excellent preparation for the 'big scale'.[1]

Legato is a MUST for every singer. Its tutelary goddess is head resonance, without which it is impossible. A professional singer needs to concentrate on maintaining and developing these three essentials.

1. breath control   2. head resonance   3. legato

It is a trinity which will lengthen the life of his voice by twenty years.

PORTAMENTO

Portamento is closely related to legato. The word comes from the Italian *portare,* to carry. Legato means the smooth linking of two or more notes, whereas portamento means a slower sliding from one note to the next. Exaggerated use is very inartistic. W. J. Henderson, in *The Art of Singing* (Dial Press, New York, 1938) writes:

> 'Portamento means the sliding of the voice through the infinitesimal gradations of tone lying between a note and the ensuing one. This languorous progress of the voice is capable of much expression when judiciously employed, but when it becomes a habit it is deplorable, because then it leads to scooping.'

---

[1] This exercise can also be adapted for use in jaw stiffness (Mouth Position, p. 42) and for acquiring head resonance (Guardian Angels, p 72.). It is analogous to the slow continuous bowing of a violin by the right hand, whilst the fingers of the left hand play a whole series of notes. Once the jaw is in motion, it should make no difference if a single note is sung, or a whole series.

So long as there are no syllables to join together, portamento in singing is the same as in a violin. The higher note should always be sung louder than the lower, whether the portamento is ascending or descending. Great care is needed in its use, for it can sound very ugly. Like *messa di voce*, it can only be mastered with the help of perfect head resonance and breath control.

A good example of how to sing portamento comes in Don Ottavio's aria in *Don Giovanni*:

The skeleton of the melody is:

In the following examples a slight portamento may be indicated when the whole phrase is sung mezza-voce:

Aria of Radames (*Aida*):

Aria of Don Ottavio (*Don Giovanni*):

A teacher should not let a student use portamento before he can use it properly. Some conductors refuse to sanction even a discreet use!

No singer can be called perfect unless he can sing piano and forte at will.

How much volume is needed for exercises? This is a relevant question to which there is a simple answer: *all exercises should be sung mezzo-forte*, except in a few special cases. Piano and forte should not be sung until the student is progressing satisfactorily. *They should only be learnt when the voice is built, and vocal technique fairly well advanced.* It depends partly on the goal: with a talented student the teacher can start much earlier. In exceptional cases it may be wise to work on piano singing from the outset—when for instance a voice has been damaged through faulty singing or illness, and has to be given special exercises by agreement with a throat specialist.

If a student tries singing forte prematurely, he tends to force, and chronic forcing will spoil the quality (see 'Quality before Volume'). A voice gets bigger little by little. It is a natural process, just as a golfer finds his muscles growing stronger through the right strokes, particularly if the practical and theoretical preparation has been sound. Some voices even get bigger with wrong training, or none at all, but these are exceptions.

Many would-be opera singers long to know if their voices can fill an opera house and ride an orchestra. In this connection I remember an interesting incident from the days when I was studying with Alexander Haydter, then one of the leading bass-baritones at the Vienna Court Opera. Haydter's voice was always beautiful, whether he was singing bass or baritone parts; he was an excellent actor, and his Beckmesser and Doctor Bartolo were inimitable. His voice was always large enough for his part, though at the time the Court Opera boasted many exceptionally big voices. Once, after he had appeared as Telramund in *Lohengrin*, which he sang with such vocal giants as Leo Slezak and Anna von Mildenburg, I asked him at a lesson to sing a high note as loudly as he had sung it the night before at the opera. He surprised me by saying: 'My friend, you ask an impossibility. I never sing as loudly in a studio as I sing on stage. Francesco d'Andrade (a famous baritone) taught me that singing should always fit the occasion and the space in which we sing. I never force; and I am never tired after a performance, even after singing strenuous parts opposite artists such as you heard yesterday, whose voices are much bigger than my own. Whatever I sing I feel able to use more voice. So when I sang yesterday with Anna von Mildenburg, I felt that I had to adjust my voice to hers. You will do the same when you have the same routine in singing on stage; but remember that only a singer with good head and chest resonance and a proper breathing technique will be safe from forcing.'

So many singers forget that in dramatic singing it is not the volume of voice that is decisive, but the skill in using one's energy. Cosima Wagner, Franz Liszt's daughter and wife of Richard Wagner, who for many years after his death educated the next generation of Wagnerian Singers, always declared: 'The real strength in dramatic singing is based not on force, but on expression.' A very wise word which I would like heartily to endorse, though naturally she was speaking of finished singers. A singer with insufficient technique would not be advised to concentrate on expression.

Another danger is to sing with the recordings of famous artists. It is certainly a temptation, but a student can get quite a wrong idea of volume through the many adjustments possible in sound reproduction. (See 'The microphone—a blessing and a danger'.)

When and How to Learn Piano Singing

Correct piano singing is always based on sufficient head resonance and no pressure on throat and neck muscles. Singers with lighter voices—such as coloratura sopranos or light lyric tenors—may often be able to sing piano without special training. But it is still one of the most difficult things to teach. Some voices may suffer if requested by a coach to sing piano without knowing how.

I would recommend the following plan of campaign:

Stage 1: The beginner sings his exercises in mezzo-forte. When the voice begins to grow quite naturally, the teacher may proceed to stage 2.

Stage 2: When a student has considerable head resonance and good breath control, he may start to sing crescendo. The exercises must be suspended if the student neglects his breath control. Crescendo exercises are the best way (though not the only way) to learn piano singing. Many teachers hold a contrary view, but for me good piano comes through crescendo and not decrescendo, largely because it is always easier to keep the throat muscles free of tension in crescendo rather than in decresendo.

Stage 3: The student sings a careful crescendo in the middle range under the watchful eyes and ears of the teacher, holding the note for as long as he has breath. He will discover to his surprise that the note ends in a perfect piano although he is still making a crescendo. If an orange is squeezed to the last, only a few drops come, although the pressure is the same.

The teacher must decide how often or how much to use this exercise, and after a time the same kind of piano tone can be produced without the detour of crescendo. A piano note learned in this way can always be reinforced to mezzo-forte and forte, and vice versa, in accordance with the rules for *messa di voce* (q.v.). Many singers can sing a good piano, but do not know how to connect it without a break to notes sung mezzo-forte or forte. An experienced teacher will always detect if the student is singing *isolated* piano notes, or notes *capable of development*. Isolated piano notes are apt to lead to a break in the voice, and may even jeopardise the forte.

Decrescendo should only be taught when a student can sing piano correctly through crescendo. Even famous singers are not always able to sing a perfect decrescendo, in the higher range, although they may sing good crescendos. They may even sing piano only in their lower range, and may resort to all sorts of tricks to avoid singing it anywhere else! Decrescendo requires perfect technique. Caruso avoided having to decrescendo on higher notes. I remember when he made his sensational debut at the Vienna Court Opera as the Duke in *Rigoletto*, the audience was a bit disappointed when he did not sing a perfect decrescendo in *La donna e mobile*, as had his famous predecessor Alessandro Bonci. Caruso compensated plentifully at the end of the aria, when he sang (and even acted!) a most original cadenza with a brilliant B natural at the end. No tenor can now resist ending *La donna e mobile* with a cadenza, regardless of whether they can sing it perfectly or not. Bonci belonged to an earlier singing generation. His star began to fade when Caruso appeared as the great master of a new period—the time of Puccini's realism and the beginning of recording. I remember as quite a young lad (but already an ardent opera connoisseur!) I heard Bonci in Vienna's second opera house in his unsurpassed performance as Almaviva in Rossini's *Barbiere*. As the great star he—and not Rosina—sang the two interpolated arias in the second act. One of them was Rodolfo's *Che gelida manina* from Puccini's *Boheme*, an opera which was still unknown in Vienna, where Leoncavallo's opera of the same name was in the repertoire of the Court Opera. I will never forget Bonci's singing of that aria, which he encored as well. It was the first and (I must confess) the last time I have heard such an unbelievably beautiful *decrescendo* on a high C. The success was tremendous; after all, nobody realised at that time that

it was sung in complete ignorance of Puccini's real style; however it was great singing art:

Here I would like to recount a true story. It happened in a
small town in Germany, which was honoured by a visit from
Richard Strauss, who had agreed to conduct a concert with the
local orchestra. During the rehearsal, Strauss challenged the first
horn-player impatiently: 'Can't you see there is piano marked
on the score? Why aren't you playing it?' 'But, Dr. Strauss',
replied the musician, 'If I could play this difficult passage in piano,
I would not be sitting here in this little town'.

*No singer can be called perfect unless he can sing piano and forte at
will,* in spite of the fact that piano and pianissimo seem to have
been blacklisted by many opera singers. The more gifted a
student and the greater his ambition, the more careful should he
be about observing the composer's wishes in piano and pianissimo.

Surprisingly enough, Toscanini frequently permitted singers to
sing certain notes and phrases forte, although the composer clearly
wanted them piano or pianissimo. In his last works particularly,
Verdi repeatedly marked pppp instead of pp. Yet certain phrases
are sometimes sung forte as a concession to inadequate technique.
Even in the ideal performance of Verdi's Requiem Mass, under
Toscanini's authentic direction, the soprano failed to sing this
exacting passage as marked.

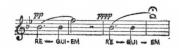

The soprano he selected for his radio performances of *Boheme* and *Traviata*[1] was also unable to sing floating head notes, which shows that even the greatest conductors are willing to make concessions. It would be inconceivable for a violinist to fail to play the end of the second movement of Mendelssohn's *Violin Concerto* in any way but as Mendelssohn wished.

After all, most arias and duos in old Italian operas—including *Rigoletto, Traviata* and *Trovatore*—are based on musical form akin to classical sonatas, symphonies and concertos. They generally have a *cavatina* (or slow movement) which precedes the brilliant *cabaletta* (or finale). The *cavatina* ends in an impressive piano or pianissimo, like the slow movement of the Mendelssohn *Concerto*.

An example of how singers often disregard the composer's explicit instructions comes in Violetta's aria in *Traviata's* Act I. It was composed in the traditional form of recitativo, and cabaletta (stretta), Verdi only abandoned tradition in his arias after his three popular operas. He clearly wished the end of the cavatina to end in piano or pianissimo—sufficient proof is the characteristic postlude, which consists of three bars played by stringed instruments:

---

[1] Later corrected and I believe transferred to records.

It is true that Verdi did not write expressly 'piano' or 'pianissimo' as at the end of the cavatina in the duo (*Rigoletto*, Act II):

But in both cases it is obvious that the singer has to end, like the orchestra, *p.* or *pp*. The duo is generally sung as the score demands, but *Ah, fors'e lui* is often sung most inartistically. Instead of ending:

it is often performed (even on records by famous singers—hence the bad effect on young students) as follows:

The soprano then tries to force a high E flat in forte against the orchestra's forte at the end of the aria. (Cf. 'Coloratura', chapter 4, p. 115.) The great Violettas I have had the privilege of hearing, which include Lilly Lehmann, Marcella Sembrich, Frieda Hempel and Selma Kurz, closed the aria with an effective trill:

Has a perfect trill gone out of vogue as well? (See 'Staccato and Trill'.)

We seldom hear the deeply affecting *arioso* of Violetta's *Addio del passato* sung as the composer wished, i.e. with *un fil di voce* (a thread of voice), three bars before marking *morendo* (dying away). Yet on records and on the radio, reputable singers try and end it with a theatrical forte, thus:

It is always easier to imitate bad habits than the technical perfection of great artists!

It would be going too far astray to quote more typical failures in piano and pianissimo singing, particularly in opera. But a soprano, who cannot sing Pamina's *Ach, ich fühl's* (*Zauberflöte*) with floating head-notes in mezza voce and piano would be well advised to stay away from the role.

Yet what can a teacher reply when a student asks, 'Why do I have to work so hard to sing piano, when Mr. X or Miss Y of the Met. cannot sing this or that phrase in piano?' The answer certainly calls for a lot of diplomacy! He could say: 'Mr. X or Miss Y are well-known singers whose shortcomings are overlooked because of their many other virtues. But it is not safe to assume that they would always be overlooked.'

I have never allowed a student to sing an important audition unless he has already learned to sing piano and pianissimo. Irene Jessner owed her success to this quality in her singing. She was thirtieth in a row of highly selected candidates for her audition at the Metropolitan. She sang the Nile Aria from *Aida*, and her high C in smooth piano at once won her the admiration of the late Arthur Bodansky (Conductor) and Edward Johnson, then General Manager of the Met. It was a decisive factor in the award of a three-year contract. She is now teaching at the Royal

Acadamy of Music, Toronto, after sixteen years at the Met. Her pupil, Miss Teresa Stratas, won the Met. 'Auditions of the Air' in 1959, and was similarly praised for her floating head-notes.

Incorrect and exaggerated piano singing may, of course, endanger good forte singing. The old Italian singing-masters liked to use the word *ponticello* (little bridge). Piano and forte are like two banks of a river: *ponticello* describes the easiest and only direct communication between the two banks. All singers should aim at a placement which enables their notes to increase to forte and diminish to piano and pianissimo without any sacrifice of tonal beauty.

THE FORGOTTEN ART OF MESSA DI VOCE

Because of the resemblance in sound, the term MESSA DI VOCE is sometimes confused with MEZZA VOCE, which of course means something quite different. *Mezza voce* means singing with half the power of the voice, whilst *messa di voce* is a technical term applied to the art of swelling or diminishing the tone by imperceptible gradation from the softest attainable piano to full volume, and vice versa. Mancini explains it as follows: 'It is the art of giving any note its gradation, starting with almost a thread of voice and then reinforcing it proportionately to the greatest power to which it can develop, then taking it back with the same gradation that has been used in going from soft to loud.'

At first, exercises for *messa di voce* should only be sung within a very small compass, and never too high. The mouth-position is very important. When the note begins, the mouth should only be opened a little, but as the note is reinforced, the mouth opening gradually gets wider. A stiff chin can be a great obstacle. If a singer masters *messa di voce*, and makes it his chief daily exercise, he will find he can achieve all the effects he wishes.

The 'big scale' recommended by Lilly Lehmann as a daily exercise also belongs to the art of *messa di voce*. But—no singer should start working on it before he is guided by the two guardian angels of the voice—head resonance and breath control! It is much easier to describe than to sing. Nowadays the heavier and more dramatic the voice the less it is expected. But ideally all voices should be able to do it.

COLORATURA SINGING OF AGILITY

The florid or coloratura style was a natural consequence of the technical virtuosity of great singers before and during the period when Handel was active as an operatic composer. Just as piano and violin virtuosi long for brilliance as well as expressiveness and beauty of tone, singing virtuosi want opportunities to show their mastery of florid singing. At one time, numerous virtuosi on the flute, clarinet, oboe, horn, trumpet and even trombone gave their own concerts at the great music centres. Compositions were written for the various instruments—even by masters such as Mozart and Beethoven. It became customary to interpolate an improvised passage in which the virtuoso could show off his virtuosity (e.g. the composed cadenza of Beethoven's *Emperor Concerto*). Small wonder that the singers wanted to shine as well!

The great *castrati* were quick to take full advantage of their abnormal make-up. Possessing female-sounding voices in strong male bodies, they could astound their audience with almost endless breath and skill in florid singing. In Handel's time particularly, every opera singer had to have a thorough mastery of this style. It was long before composers abandoned such writing for all except high soprano voices. It almost became a rule that whenever a soprano appeared in an operatic part in which she became insane, she had to sing coloratura.[1] Nobody knows the connection between coloratura and insanity (!), but the soprano who

[1] *Lucia di Lammermoor* (Donizetti), *Linda di Chamonunix* (Donizetti), *Catherine* (L'Etoile du Nord) by Meyerbeer, *Ophelia* (Hamlet by Thomas), *Elvira* (I Puritani), etc.

was able to excel at the florid style because of her easy floating light-weight voice and skilled use of head resonance received as permanent reward the title of 'coloratura'.

The modern teacher has to decide whether florid singing should be learnt only by future coloratura singers, or to some extent by all voices. My opinion is that they should all learn it, at least in exercises: and this for the same reason that people take dancing lessons—not to become dancers but to acquire grace. A singer who sings fluent scales will be able to achieve a better tone than those who can only produce notes of a certain volume and find a smooth legato difficult. It will also greatly assist the singing of quick musical phrases, as demanded by many operatic parts. Agility exercises are an excellent remedy for stiffness of the jaw, which obstructs a floating and easy tone (see Mouth Position).

The younger the singer, the easier it will be to train him in agility, even if the voice later develops into a heavier dramatic voice. It was an advantage for dramatic singers like Lilly Lehmann and Lilian Nordica to have sung coloratura parts such as Lucia, Gilda, Filina (*Mignon*) and the Queen (*Les Huguenots*) in their early years, later to excel in dramatic parts such as Isolde.

It is really a question of musical education. It is quite unthinkable for an orchestral player not to know how to play fast scales on his instrument (unless it is heavy brass), or for a pianist to be unable to play any sort of scale. In other words, agility exercises are fundamental to the mastery of any instrument, including singing.

In the early stages, the teacher must decide how much can be undertaken. The initial steps should be taken in the first lessons when the teacher shows the student how to place notes well, and link them smoothly. A student should not start singing scales until he can master exercises employing a more limited range, which gives him a smooth legato. Even in the daily practice of more advanced singers, it is unwise to sing scales covering more than one octave until the voice is sufficiently warmed up. A warmly expressive operatic voice may even be jeopardised by too many exercises in florid singing. It is obvious that it calls for different principles than those used in expressive singing: the general placement of coloraturas is quite different from that of voices suited for lyric and dramatic singing (as mentioned in the chapter on Covering, covering helps many types of singing, but can be a hindrance for coloraturas).

I recommend the following daily exercises to students and singers alike:

The teacher must decide on the suitable range. Start by using the vowel AY (as in pay) and then use AH. The subsequent choice of vowels depends on the needs and the ability of the student.

In all florid exercises, and especially in scale passages, a student should never *push* the highest notes in ascending scales in his effort to accentuate them. (See chapter 3.) It is better to make a gradual crescendo so that the notes indicated in the following example are sung with the same energy and volume. It is a good idea to open the mouth gradually as the top note is approached:

This exercise and those following should only be sung by

advanced students, above all by coloraturas. Notes marked**
should be accented.

It does not matter greatly if a student sings a multitude of
different exercises or a group of selected ones, constantly repeated.
It depends on the degree of musicality. There comes to mind the
well-known story of Porpora[1] and his student Cafarelli[2]. When
Porpora accepted him as a very young student, he wrote on a
single page some scales, diatonic and chromatic, ascending and
descending, and various intervals; thirds, fourths, fifths etc., as
well as exercises for embellishments. The story tells how Cafarelli
worked under his master's guidance for six years, singing nothing
more than these exercises. It is clear that they also worked for

[1] Porpora, Nicola (Naples, 1686–1766), a famous teacher and composer who boasted
three extraordinary pupils: Farinelli, Senesino and Caferelli.

[2] Cafarelli (real name Gaetano Majorano (1703–1783), famous castrato, died as Duca
di S. Dorato.

perfect articulation, pronunciation and declamation, but the nucleus of study remained the exercises, written on a single page. After six meticulous years, the master said: 'Go, my son, you are the greatest singer in the world.' Whether or not this is legend or clever invention, the fact remains that the best results are obtained by working a couple of cleverly selected exercises day by day, provided that the work is extremely careful. What matters is HOW they are sung, not how many. There are a multitude of useful exercises in volumes by Concone, Bordogni, Lutgen, etc.

As there are three types of light coloratura singers:

1. High coloratura sopranos (Queen of the Night, Zerbinetta);

2. Coloratura soubrettes (Susanna, Zerlina etc.);

3. Lyric coloraturas (Lucia, Gilda, Elvira (*Puritani*), Violetta (*Traviata*), Amina (*Sonnambula*) who can also sing some lyric-dramatic parts,

the teacher has to be very sure where a student's talents lie. Too much work in agility may even jeopardise the real destination of the voice. In many operas, e.g. *Don Giovanni*, Bellini's *Norma*, and the earlier Verdi operas, the dramatic soprano has also to sing coloratura passages. She has to be able to change her note-placement convincingly when it comes to coloraturas within a dramatic aria as in:

An especially difficult task for modern sopranos are the kind of phrases which occur in Bellini's *Norma*. In an outbreak of violent emotion, the deeply offended Norma attacks Pollione—in coloraturas. Bellini expressively demands 'con tutta forza' (with all possible strength) . . .

But this is an exceptional part, and very few singers are able to do it justice today. The instrumental coloraturas at the end of Leonore's aria in *Fidelio* are often inadequately sung, even by famous sopranos:

The coloraturas of Donna Anna in *Don Giovanni* are also very difficult. The singer has to show off her dramatic power and expression, in her *scene* in Act I, and sing coloraturas like these in the second act:

A perfectly equipped dramatic soprano has to work hard to master these, whilst a coloratura soprano who wants to sing, say, Violetta in *Traviata* has to sing expressive and even dramatic phrases as in Act II. It needs perfect vocal technique to overcome these difficulties.

Sopranos who are trained for coloratura, staccato and other singing 'fireworks' often overdo their embellishments. Since many of them cannot end an aria on a full-sounding high note or a good trill, they sing some note above high C in forte. Because of their hardness and their artificiality, I call these notes 'electric bell' notes. They are not only tasteless, but harsh and inhuman.[1]

---

[1] The fact that Joan Sutherland uses such notes, especially as Lucia in *Lucia di Lammermoor* should not be misunderstood. She is a mature singer with an exceptional high range and above all she is a star (she can sing whatever she likes). A young girl may harm her voice very much by imitating these high notes in forte.

They are also dangerous for the quality of the voice in the middle range. But it is a vicious circle: the singer realises she can make little impression with her lower notes, so she takes refuge in her beloved high notes, although they are more effective than beautiful. An average audience accepts them with noisy rapture. By overstraining the voice too often, the voice suffers—and the singer, like an addict, clings to them all the more. It is every singer's fate: as soon as she and her public realise there is a deficiency, the more formidable becomes the menace of the many singers eagerly waiting to take her place.

Light lyric tenors who also use a great deal of agility have little chance to show themselves off except in parts such as Don Ottavio (*Don Giovanni*), Nemorino (*Elisir*), Ernesto (*Don Pasquale*) and Almaviva (*Barbiere di Siviglia*).

Coloratura singing is generally more difficult for lower voices; but some excellent baritones master parts like Figaro (Rossini), Malatesta (*Don Pasquale*), etc. Many mezzo-sopranos have successfully reasserted their rights to the originally mezzo role of Rosina (*Barbiere*) wresting it from the coloraturas, who had managed to add it to their not very rich repertoire of roles!

STACCATO AND TRILL

'. . . she sings the trill slowly and I like it, since it will be pure and clearer when she sings it faster. In any case it is easier to sing faster.'

MOZART in a letter from Munich, October 1, 1777.

Staccato singing is used in particular by coloratura sopranos. It is better not to start staccato exercises too soon. The time to begin is when a student can sing a good legato and has the full range of the voice. Premature exercises are dangerous because of the danger of a stiff jaw. Light female voices obviously find it easier to reach high notes in staccato than in legato. But notes that can only be reached in staccato cannot help general vocal development. High notes should first be sung in legato, so that the right way to sing them can be embodied in the voice. Legato notes can be developed: staccato notes cannot. A singer should not run away with the idea that she 'has' certain notes because she can sing them staccato. Even the famous phrase with the high F in *Magic Flute* which Mozart wrote to please his sister-in-law, Josephine Hofer, the first 'Queen of the Night', will never be completely safe unless it can first be sung as an exercise in legato.

Some coloratura sopranos achieve immense skill in staccato. The effect can be astonishing, but if used too much it may be won at the price of smooth legato. Sooner or later their voices will lack beauty. As in piano or violin playing, it is not staccato or pizzicato which moves an audience, so much as a soulful legato. Unfortunately, a vicious circle is created in which such singers realise that they have overworked their staccato, and use it all the more to compensate for loss of legato skill. Staccatos are technical tricks rightly called vocal acrobatics. An audience wearies of them if they are used too much, but used with artistry and economy, they never fail to create a sensation.

A well-known New York music critic, Pitts Sanborn, once attended a recital by a famous coloratura who made too much show of this facility, and he described her not as a *coloratura*, but as a *staccato* soprano . . .

Exercises to develop a good trill should only be started when legato singing has been mastered. The lighter the voice, the sooner trill exercises can begin. It is best to teach them first mezzo forte and even forte, for to sing them piano is more difficult. It is strange that lyric dramatic and dramatic voices often have a better natural trill than many coloraturas.

The trill went out of vogue in the U.S. for a very simple reason. In a successful career of more than twenty years, Lilly Pons has hardly ever used a trill, so that multitudes of young coloraturas think it is unnecessary and do not study it. To make up for it, they insert too many runs, staccato passages and other embellishments into their cadenzas. In 1777, nearly two hundred years ago, Giambattista Mancini was deploring the neglect of the trill:

> 'That the trill is neglected today, although it is clearly indispensable, can only cause amazement. Why is it neglected? It is never the fault of the student . . . When singers cannot trill, they say that nature has been partial and has not provided them with a trill . . . I consider they are mistaken because through patient study it can be acquired. If I am asked for precise rules to assist the execution of the trill, I can only say that a *positive rule does not exist.*'

Mancini was probably referring to male singers, since in the time of Mozart and Rossini it is hardly possible to think of coloratura sopranos and other women singers without trills. Yet his remarks show that the old masters had no recipe for teaching it. Mozart's comment at the head of this chapter provides the only sure way of studying a trill, i.e. by singing it slowly and then increasing speed.

COVERING AND COLOURING
Don't confuse them!

Opinions about covering and colouring vary greatly, even amongst good performers and teachers. They often accept the idea of colouring, but deny the existence of covering, and do not know how it is done, unaware of the great advantages of a technique which for many is a primary principle. The following differentiation may help to clarify the confusion between the two terms:

1. (*a*) *Covering* is a technical device which helps to give greater intensity and beauty to the transitional notes, i.e.

IN SOPRANOS AND TENORS

IN BARITONES AND BASSES

It can also help in reaching well-placed high notes. It can help lyric voices to sing dramatic arias, and sometimes even dramatic parts, without coming to any harm: e.g. coloratura sopranos can master *Butterfly*, or lyric baritones can sing *Rigoletto*. It has also been used to assist a tenor who had been erroneously singing baritone.

(*b*) *Colouring* gives the desired colour to *any* note in the singer's range. Some teachers believe that all notes, particularly in the middle range, require the same placement. This is held by many baritones and basses, who make the mistake of forming a general rule from their own practice. Admittedly all notes in the middle range have a main centre on the hard palate, and the singer (and speaker) always feels a certain vibration there. But a well-trained singer can feel how his note-placement changes from note to note in the direction of the soft palate.

Covering means remaining deliberately at the same placement for the transitional notes, instead of going back from note to note towards the soft palate, as for the notes which precede and follow. It cannot be understood if all notes in the middle range are thought to have a single placement.

Very good description of perception of a High Soprano (according to Lilly Lehmann
"Meine Gesangskunst" Verlag der Zukunft, Berlin, 1909).

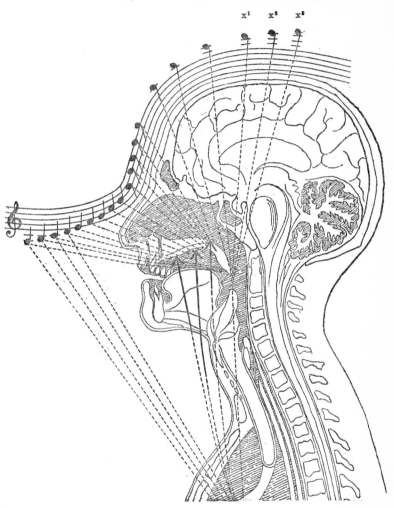

The highest notes x^1 x^2 x^3 should not be placed and felt at the palate. If forced, they
sound shrill and unfeminine, more or less like an electric bell. They are comparable
to flagiolet notes on a string instrument : they must sound sweet but never forceful.

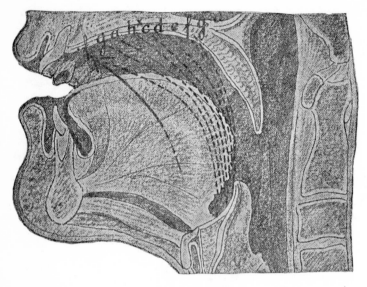

Soprano, Tenor. Not Covered.
*No space for B and C.

2. *How to Learn Covering*

The teacher must be able to demonstrate transitional notes both covered and uncovered. It should not be studied until floating notes can be sung in the middle range with an open, unconstricted throat, as covering involves the coordination of different muscle-groups. Covered notes are generally darker than uncovered ones: AH will sound more like OH, AIR (affair) will sound like AY (pay). In my own experience the following exercise is very effective both with beginners and practising singers:

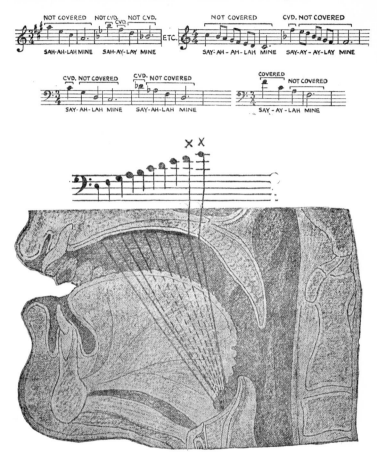

BASS, BARITONE. Not Covered.
**Not good placement for the average Baritone.

An experienced singer will sometimes make deliberate exceptions. I remember Caruso's first performance as the Duke in *Rigoletto* at the Vienna Court Opera. In the quartet *Bella Figlia del l'Amore* he always sang the F (a) MO (re) covered, as the following A flat, while at the end of the phrase he purposely sang the last F with a floating, open tone. The effect was immense, and he had to repeat his initial phrases before the quartet could proceed!

The note before the covered note has to be a 'free' note (to avoid saying 'open') i.e. as lightly sung as possible. Sometimes it is very difficult to follow this rule, for instance when the last note in the middle range is a dark one, and the covered note has to be sung in a light AH, as in

In spite of the EE vowel ('mich'), the E flat has to be sung uncovered, with the mouth as open as possible. On the other hand, the A flat of 'heissen' should be covered; the Ah of the diphthong 'heissen' needs a darker colour, so that it sounds 'heussen'. These are the exceptions.

Covering without perfect breath control is dangerous. As covered notes have more intensity than others, they need more preparation i.e., greater support from the diaphragm. Sometimes singers who have almost mastered the technique give it up because it is too much effort. Just before a covered note is sung, the diaphragm should be reinforced, just as the arms are braced before taking hold of a heavy object. The premature decay of a voice is often due to a lack of this preparation.

Danger of Overcovering. Basses and contraltos have a tendency to overcover the middle range, so that their transition notes are not free of tension. In many old records, Caruso can be heard deliberately exaggerating the lightness of the notes before the transitional notes, so as to avoid this fault. Some singers cannot reach high notes easily because they sing their transitional notes

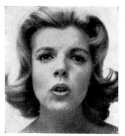

TRAVIATA

Ah, forsè lui

E Strano

Ah, fors-è lui

A quele' amor!

Cro-ce

Croce de-lizia

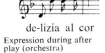

de-lizia al cor

Expression during after play (orchestra)

sempre

Ri-tro-vi - - -

Facial expression particularly of the eyes

General Exercises

too openly, or darken (i.e. overcover) too much. Covering is like tuning a radio: a slight miscalculation, and the sound is ugly, a slight correction, and the perfect sound is obtained.

Covering is essential in forte, but a positive hindrance in piano and mezza voce, and also in coloratura singing. That is why the forte notes of some lyric tenors sound strained: they try to use the same open production in forte as they use so successfully in mezza voce and piano.

Involuntary Covering. Singers who have never learnt to cover sometimes sing a good covered note. This is because the note immediately preceding the covered note is a word on AH in the middle range, followed by a word with Oh on F or G (for sopranos and tenors). If the singer has good breath-control the G will sound very good, quite different from other G's which have to be sung on AH. It is strange that even good artists pay no attention to these facts, but make up their mind that certain notes are easier for them than others.

Covered Tone on Records is an advantage. When recording first began, only darker voices could be well recorded, which was one of the chief reasons for Caruso's great success with it. But even nowadays with improved recording technique, an open forte in the higher range will not sound well, although the mezza voce (piano, pianissimo) of a lyric tenor of the Schipa/Tagliavini type will sound perfectly all right, even when sung in a light, uncovered way.

Continuity with the upper range can be obtained by changing over from covering to colouring at the right moment. The process is difficult to describe, but basses and baritones tend to equate high notes and covered notes by the use of colouring. Using plenty of head resonance, a good singer will discover when he changes from covering to colouring. A baritone may be able to reach a good G by keeping the same position for high notes and covered notes, though he will probably sound tenorish when he reaches A flat (as in the Prologue to *Pagliacci*). This is perfectly normal. Sopranos and tenors often colour the notes above covered notes.

The only real way of learning covering is by studying it with a teacher who believes in it and knows how to teach it. A book of hints on 'How to become a Raphael' would not make anyone a good painter. The real work is done in the teacher's studio, where the pupil contributes his talent, and the teacher his knowledge.

3. *Colouring*

Single notes or whole phrases can be sung in a lighter or darker colour. Even a whole part can be treated in this way, just as a painter or stage designer decides on a tonality to suit the general mood of picture or a play. A baritone who sings Figaro in *Barbiere* normally uses a lighter colour than he would for the four demoniacal counterparts in Offenbach's *Tales of Hoffmann*. He will 'apply' this colour[1] without affecting his voice or his general technique. It is also very useful in helping operatic partners (e.g. Aida and Radames) to blend well. It is not recommended for students whose technique is still in formation. Conductors and coaches can do harm if they encourage young performers too much, as good colouring needs a special flair, and they do not always have it. Great composers often have it naturally: the dark mood of Elvira's E flat aria in *Don Giovanni* is intensified by Mozart's instinctive use of dark woodwind.

Covering and colouring are both ways of refining tone, and should not be systematically learnt until a student sings in a natural, unstrained way. Caruso was a great master of colouring and varied his tone-colour in arias recorded at the same time, always retaining his own distinctive timbre.

---

[1] By head resonance, q.v.

CHAPTER 5

CORRECTING FAULTS

VIBRATO A VIRTUE—TREMOLO A VICE

Vibrato means a regular oscillation of one note, based on the laws of acoustics. It is a quality of a healthy, trained voice. No other instrument has this natural 'swinging' of notes. String-players learn to make a vibrato in a legato phrase by regularly oscillating the strings with the fingers of the left hand. But in singing there are no special exercises.

Tremolo is caused when not one but two different notes are heard, intermittently and with variable intensity. It can be caused in many ways:

1. Emotional excitement,
2. Overworked voice, general fatigue,
3. Defective technique, particularly poor breath control,
4. Excessive pressure on the larynx,
5. Nervous system out of order,
6. Vocal cords out of order,
7. Symptom of senility.

The sooner a tremolo is noticed, the better. There are many ways of curing it, depending on the cause: often a good rest helps. Sometimes a doctor is needed. It is a serious warning, and a singer should heed it at once, as it prevents smooth singing.[1]

[1] George Bernard Shaw wrote of a performance of *Cavalleria Rusticana* in October, 1891: '. . . Signor Brombara is, I fear, incurable, and must look for fame to countries where the tremolo is popular.' He adds one of his characteristically wise comments on singing: 'Would it be an impertinence on my part, by the bye, to remark that tremolo and vibrato are not synonymous terms? There is not even the most distant relationship or resemblance between them. One is a defect of the gravest kind; the other is one of the most precious graces a dramatic singer can acquire—if it can be acquired at all . . .'

Flat and sharp singing generally occurs in the transitional notes to the high range, and in phrases with semitones.

A musician who plays an instrument without fixed keys produces impure intonation because of an imperfect ear, or a faulty technique. Singers rarely have a perfect instrument as well as a finished technique, and difficulties in intonation are bound to occur. Even reputable singers are not always able to sing on pitch. Contemporary critics report that Isabella Angela Colbran (1785–1845), the famous contralto, sometimes sang 'excruciatingly out of tune'. Her father was court musician to the King of Spain, her teacher was the soprano castrato Girolamo Crescentini (1762–1846), one of the last great representatives of *bel canto*, and her husband was Rossini himself. Beyond all doubt Madame Colbran was a remarkable and well-trained singer—yet she sang out of tune, nobody knows why. Contemporary reports have it that singers in the first German operas (e.g. the première of *Fidelio*) also had this defect. Here the reason is easier to find. Most of the male singers of this period were actors with too little musical training behind them, and it was not surprising that they found intonation difficult in such dramatic roles. Another famous singer, Theodore Reichmann, leading baritone for years at the Vienna Court Opera, was notorious for bad intonation—yet Wagner chose him from among countless fine baritones to create the part of Amfortas in the Bayreuth *Parsifal*.

The list could be greatly extended, but it would only go to show that successful singing needs so many different qualities that certain failings have often to be overlooked. That does not mean that students can treat it lightly. *Quod licet Jovi, non licet bovi,* says the Latin proverb—(What is all right for Jupiter is not all right for an ox). I hope the proverb will be taken in good part!

The term 'flat singing' is used by laymen who never recognise any other kind. Many claim to be disturbed by it, but one suspects that they are out to make an impression. They seldom complain about sharp singing, though this is a common fault.

Flat and sharp singing generally occur in the transitional notes to the high range, and in phrases with semitones. Singing flat has no general remedy because it can be caused in so many ways:

1. Defective ear,
2. Insufficient head resonance,
3. Over-heavy singing, hence overstrained vocal cords,
4. Physical disturbances,
5. General fatigue,
6. Senility.

1.—Defective Ear

It is sad when this afflicts otherwise fine singers. Defective hearing can often be improved by systematic study, though not invariably. The expression 'he (or she) has a good ear' is very relative, and is applied to very different faculties. It may merely mean an interest in music, or that someone can repeat a tune long after hearing it, or pick out the notes in a chord. It may mean realising if something is out of tune, whether in oneself or others, and knowing how to put it right; it may mean absolute pitch, or the power to identify the pitch of a sound, the key of a piece. Singing teachers need to hear *how* a note is sung (i.e. 'analytical' hearing). Conductors need to know if instrumentalists are playing the right notes, and if a chorus is off-pitch or out of time. The leader of a string quartet while playing will know at once if one of his partners has played a wrong note. Toscanini had a wonderful ear. He could spot wrong pronunciation by a singer in a language he had only heard spoken. He had a legendary memory for scores, a gift shared by some present-day conductors (Karajan, Steinberg, etc.). Mozart's memory and musical ear were quite phenomenal. As a boy he attended Mass with his father in the Sistine Chapel. It was Easter-time, and the singers were performing a famous *Miserere* by Allegri. This piece was held in such high esteem that the musicians were forbidden under threat of excommunication, to take the manuscript sheets out of the Chapel. The fourteen-year-old Mozart heard it once, and wrote it down from memory when he got home. The next day he went again, held the manuscript against his hat and made corrections. The affair became known, and caused much excitement. Later Mozart played the music to the Papal singer Cristofori, who pronounced it to be an exact duplicate.

So between the 'good ear' of the average person and the 'good ear' of a genius there is a considerable gap.

2.—*Insufficient Head Resonance*
Work with a good teacher is the answer.

3., 4. and 5., *over-heavy singing, fatigue* and other *physical disturbances*:
These call for a visit to the throat specialist, who will probably prescribe complete rest, after which a good teacher can help. It is important to treat the condition early. Both doctor and teacher must be implicitly obeyed.

Singing Sharp.
This is the least harmful of the two evils. Its reasons vary, but it is often caused by too much head resonance and too little breath control. A high state of excitement is also likely to cause it. A coach or conductor who continually corrects bad intonation is making a mistake and will only make matters worse. The singer may be aware that he is out of tune without being able to correct it, or he may not even hear that notes are out of tune. He will get more and more agitated if he is told 'Don't sing flat': 'Can't you hear you're singing flat?' It is as futile as saying 'Pull yourself together' to somebody who is feeling upset.

The sooner bad intonation is diagnosed, the more easily it is corrected. But if it is caused by a bad ear, then love's labour will most likely be lost!

CONSTANT HOARSENESS

Constant hoarseness in the middle register is a warning that something is wrong. A good singer nearly always has a clear speaking voice. The vocal cords should be examined by a specialist, and if nothing is physically wrong, the singer may be sure that the voice production is at fault. If high notes are sung too openly, dramatically or forcefully, they will affect the middle range. Is the middle register still hoarse even when no high notes are sung? Hoarseness will become chronic unless the notes and tone that are causing the trouble are identified, which is seldom easy to do. Like running a temperature, hoarseness is a warning, and the only remedy is to rest the voice for as long as the condition requires.

FORCING

'In the opinion of the Italians the tone of an instrument sounds beautiful only if it is not forced.'
ECKERMANN: Talks with Goethe. 3

Pushing, shouting, coughing and screaming (see Health, p. 190) are enemies of the vocal cords. Singers should see on what tiny membranes the whole of singing depends, and avoid straining their vocal cords. They could best be compared to two rubber-bands which once overstrained can never regain their former elasticity.

Pushing notes is very dangerous. The right way to open a door is to unlock it; only in emergencies should it be forced, as it does the door no good. The only way for the vocal cords to function is to let a controlled amount of inhaled air pass through them, and then prepare the correct shape for the sound, whether notes or words.

Notes should never be produced in the haphazard way of 'pop' singers. In dramatic singing, excitement and nervous strain often stops the breath from being transformed into sound. In singing higher notes, which need more muscular support, the breath is often not prepared in time, and the note is emitted by force.

Forcing will often cause persistent throat irritation. Those who habitually force often think of throat irritation as a necessary evil and ignore it. For forcing is a relative term. If two children are forced to walk for an hour, it will be harder on the younger than the elder. A robust and fully developed voice can stand up to more intensive use for a longer time than a delicate voice. That some singers can force for a long time without ill-effects may easily be misinterpreted. They are simply able to take it. Singers with strong bodies tend to force more than those of smaller build. A healthy singer will only consult a specialist when he has no other choice, where a more delicate singer would not have waited.

Hence the worst result of forcing—nodules on the vocal cords—shows itself more in strong male singers than in others. The usual cure for an often fatal symptom is to stop talking and singing entirely, whereupon it may disappear. If it has grown too big, only an operation can help. It is a very dangerous one, as the slightest injury to one of the cords may permanently damage it, and a surgeon has to work under great difficulties with a long thin instrument. Fortunately, nodules are rare, but singers should be quite clear about the extreme consequences of forcing. It is better to sing too little rather than too much. Nothing is more tragic than to have acquired technique, reputation and plenty of opportunity, and then to discover that the voice is no longer in good condition.

To look after the vocal cords is not to pamper them.

CHAPTER 6

WARNING AGAINST DANGERS

MORE HASTE, LESS SPEED

'Chi va piano—va sano
Chi va piano—va lontano'
(Italian proverb expressing same idea.)

Nothing is more dangerous than to be in a hurry . . . start studying to soon . . . singing words too soon . . . singing concerts too soon . . . singing a role too soon.

Here is an apt story about the rascally Till Eulenspiegel: Till was walking along when the driver of an old carriage stopped him, and asked how long it would take to drive to the next town. Till looked at the poor condition of the vehicle, and the miserable old mare, and said: 'If you drive slowly, you can reach the town in an hour.' 'You fool' came the answer, 'I'm in a hurry.' 'Oh, if you hurry, I don't know how long it will take,' Till called after the hurriedly departing carriage. Later he came upon driver, carriage and horse, lying in a ditch. 'I told you, you could reach the town in an hour if you drove slowly, friend!'

How many ambitious singers-to-be end up in a ditch because of their hurry!

BETWEEN SCYLLA AND
CHARYBDIS

'Dum vitant stulti vitia in contraria corrunt.'
HORACE, Satires, 1, 2, 24.
(A fool avoids errors and runs into opposite ones.)

A teacher must be able to guide a singer through the dangerous strait of Scylla and Charybdis. He teaches a brilliant high range, and the student sings big, shining high notes, but the lower and middle range lose colour and evenness. When they finally match, pronunciation is difficult. Or teacher and student go all out for good piano notes, and find they do not match the forte; or concentrate so much on breath control that the student gets a stiff lower jaw; acquires dramatic intensity, but loses legato. It is never good to concentrate too much on one operation.

WRONG CONCLUSIONS

> 'Oh, most lame and impotent conclusion!'
>
> SHAKESPEARE; *Othello*, II.

Wrong conclusions are dangerous in any field, but in singing they can be disastrous. A famous singer may have an awkward mouth position, although he sings beautifully. A student might easily assume that part of his success was due to his mouth position. If he imitated it, he would ruin his placement and perhaps endanger his voice. For the singer he is imitating sings well not BECAUSE of this, but IN SPITE of it. Caruso was one of the greatest singers of all time not BECAUSE of excessive smoking, but IN SPITE of it.

Some singers say that though they never cover their transition notes, they have easy, ringing high notes. This does not mean that they have an excellent high range BECAUSE they sing their transitional notes carelessly: they are lucky to have good high notes IN SPITE of their negligence.

Some false conclusions injure others beside the singer. A successful artist may consult a doctor if he has difficulty in certain passages, or if his high notes lose brilliance or ease. The doctor finds nothing wrong, and thinks the cause may be nervous disturbance or something similar. If the singer cannot consult his own teacher, he goes to somebody who can prescribe a remedy, and sings splendidly at his next performance. Is this BECAUSE of the exercises he has been given, or IN SPITE of them?

If he thinks he gave a good performance during a trying period, he will say IN SPITE. If he thinks the exercises were responsible, he will say BECAUSE, and recommend the person who has helped him. His enthusiasm may lead young singers to study with someone whose only real art is that of persuasion. Plenty of teachers and coaches can help professional singers over their difficulties, without necessarily being good at voice training.

False conclusions in singing are quite limitless. I will mention one further example: the baritone who can sing top notes with a brilliant tenor quality. This does not make him a tenor any more than one swallow makes a summer. Many people go to work with a high temperature: they recover not BECAUSE they failed to take precautions, but IN SPITE of it!

KNOW YOUR LIMITS

Systematic training can expand and extend a voice, which normally grows with the possessor from seventeen to twenty-five: but like all rules, this is limited. The more delicate the voice, the sooner will the limit be reached which in no circumstances should be overstepped. Lily Pons was wise not to try and enlarge her delicate coloratura voice by forcing it in any way. A precious silk dress will be damaged if it gets wet, though many stronger materials come to no harm in any kind of weather. Some voices may safely be used in dramatic roles, and even in speaking parts; others react adversely as soon as a heavy aria has been sung. Adelina Patti had a small voice, but was able to sing Aida, which she studied with Verdi. Marcella Sembrich, Nellie Melba and others were able to sing lyric-dramatic roles without any ill effects.

THE DANGER OF TOO MUCH VERSATILITY

Modern singers have to be versatile, but therein lies a risk. It makes complete success in any one field extremely difficult.

Deliberately or unconsciously, many students work against a teacher by wanting to do something which does not suit them, or by accepting an engagement which is beyond them for the sake of experience. It is better to lose an opportunity rather than take a risk which can have bad consequences. Versatility is a necessary attribute for secondary roles and players of small parts— but who studies singing only to sing small parts?

QUALITY BEFORE VOLUME

It is better to sing well-placed notes with a small volume than to sing loudly with a strained sound. Each note has a limit beyond which the beauty disappears, and only the volume remains. The lighter the voice, the sooner will its beauty disappear if it is reinforced. Run your fingers over the piano keys, and you can get an idea of its tone: a skilled pianist can produce the same quality of sound even when he plays loudly. The dividing line between sound and noise is very slight.

Some students are convinced that they have beautiful voices however loudly they sing: they have been given a magic hearing-aid which makes them believe their voices are much better than they sound to others, particularly connoisseurs. It is very natural to be biassed in this way.

Female singers must be especially careful in order not to lose the mellowness of their middle range. Once lost, that beautiful natural softness cannot be regained. But it means so much, above all in women's voices, as Lear says about Cordelia 'Her voice was ever soft, gentle and low. An excellent thing in women.'

CHAPTER 7

CLASSIFYING AND SOMETIMES RETRAINING

LYRIC OR DRAMATIC

Some singers have outstanding dramatic ability and would un-doubtedly make successful actors were they to choose that profession. Others are talented for the musical side, while a third group have a God-given voice but no marked dramatic or musical ability. These last manage to learn their parts tolerably well and are generally content to show off their voices to the best advantage. They often fail to understand why conductors or connoisseurs prefer singers with less brilliant voices but great musical or dramatic ability. Those who are good at acting and have a good enough voice for dramatic parts are indeed fortunate, while singers who have voice, talent, *and* appearance are thrice blessed. Lauritz Melchior possessed all three: even his love of big-game hunting and imposing appearance fitted the physical needs of roles such as Siegfried. What would have happened had Melchior had the lyric voice of Tagliavini, and Tagliavini with his smallish body the talent and ambition of an heroic tenor? Nature is generally wise and judicious, and gives singers the right body for their parts. But Melchior voices and temperaments do sometimes have a Tagliavini appearance (e.g. the late heroic tenor, Carl Burian). The same is also true of women singers.

Gifted young singers are constantly being persuaded to undertake dramatic roles too soon, because of their appearance or the size of their voices. Roles such as Brunhilde, Isolde, Salome, Elektra, Fidelio, Siegfried, Tristan, Wotan, Hans Sachs and Otello —to mention a few—should not be studied, let alone performed, before the singer is at least thirty. Even roles in 'veristic' operas like *Cavalleria, Pagliacci, Tosca,* etc., should not be approached by inexperienced singers. American singers suffer from having to make debuts in over-large halls; this unavoidable fact ought to restrict the choice of operatic parts. The great heroic voices of the past, for instance Herman Winkelmann (1849–1912), the first Parsifal, and Albert Niemann (1839–1917) made their debuts respectively in Sondershausen and Halle, in opera houses which hold between 800 to 1,000. The orchestras were also much smaller, and young singers could acquire stage routine without forcing their voices. It is not surprising that they were able to preserve the beauty of their voices for years. To object to the fact that we are now able to reinforce voices and even entire performances artificially through a microphone is misleading, and points to many false conclusions (see 'Blessing and Danger of the Microphone'). Kerstin Flagstad sang dramatic parts such as Isolde, Brunhilde and Alceste on the stage and on records in her later fifties at the end of a most successful career. Her secret was that she began in light opera and for years sang much lighter roles. Amalia Materna (1845–1918), Wagner's own choice for Brunhilde and Kundry, also began on the stage in light opera: I was able to admire her ringing high notes (her top C was as beautiful as it was powerful) at well over sixty. Gustav Hypolith Roger (1815–1879) sang lyrical tenor roles for ten years at the Opéra Comique before creating the strenuous part of Meyerbeer's Prophete. Lilly Lehmann (1842–1929) sang almost the entire repertoire of soubrette, coloratura and lyric roles before singing Fidelio and Norma, and was over forty before she came to

Brunhilde and Isolde.[1] Although she did not have a naturally big voice, she sang these roles with incomparable mastery, thanks to her head resonance and perfect breath control. Small wonder that such artists could conserve their vocal powers much longer than the average opera singer.

Just as boxing has its lightweights and heavyweights, so there are lyric and dramatic singers. But in singing there are no commissions to decide on the category. It is impossible in artistic spheres to establish dividing lines and specifications: there would be too many borderline cases. But just as it is possible to progress from lightweight to middleweight, so during his career a singer can advance from one type of singing to another, the determining factor being his set of vocal cords. This decides whether he is a lyric or dramatic singer. Normally, more delicate vocal cords are better adapted for lyric parts. But thorough training can strengthen them to such an extent that their possessor can safely tackle more dramatic roles. Caruso's first teacher, Vergine, nicknamed him 'Signor Vento' (Mr. Wind), as in those early days his voice was weak and small.

The more mature a young singer's voice and technique, the more easily will he master dramatic parts when he comes to sing them. A well-spent year of study will prolong the life of a voice by many years. The trouble is that it is tempting and often easier for a dramatically gifted young singer to sing a dramatic aria or part than a bel canto aria, and may lead to quicker success. This 'success' can be disastrous for the future (see 'Success sometimes a danger'). Just as make-up hides pallor or skin blemishes,

[1] It is interesting that Lilly Lehmann did not sing *Isolde* in public until she had sung the first act continuously through seven times without an audience. Only when it was quite effortless did she sing the whole part in public. Over a period of 25 years I was able to hear this incomparable artist repeatedly in her great roles, Norma, Donna Anna, Fidelio, Isolde, Brunhilde, Constanze (*Entführung*). She sang *Traviata* (another of her best roles) when she was approaching sixty. From her debut in 1865 as the First Boy in *Magic Flute* in Prague, she sang no less than 170 roles in 119 operas. She was a genius in her field, and won the admiration of all musicians with whom she came into contact, from Wagner and Verdi to Gustav Mahler.

dramatic accents often conceal vocal defects or shortcomings. But as make-up cannot remove the reason for the pallor or the blemishes, *dramatic accents cannot correct the weaknesses in the voice.* The singer of lyric arias can concentrate on producing good tone and legato because he does not have to work himself up to a high pitch of emotion, nor expend energy on dramatic gestures and violent movements. In a highly dramatic part, the whole singing apparatus is under strain, and only an experienced singer can function properly under such exacting circumstances. If one is talking in a foreign language, it is much easier to talk quietly in the living-room than argue heatedly in a courtroom at the top of one's voice. That is the extent of the difference between singing a lyric aria in a concert hall and singing a dramatic role on the stage.

It may help if I quote a few cases from my own experience. I had a pupil at the Vienna Conservatory, who was pretty and graceful; even in everyday life she was coquettish and alluring. No wonder that she was repeatedly advised to study Carmen. She would clearly be a great success, said her friends. As her teacher I had a difficult time dissuading her. Nature had given her a voice suitable for lyric roles such as Pamina in *Magic Flute* or Mimi in *Boheme*. I comforted her as best I could, assuring her that when her voice had matured and she had had more experience, she would very likely be able to tackle a difficult role like Carmen. She was wise and listened to my advice. She has since developed into a most successful singer who sings some dramatic parts as well.

Another difficult case arose with a singer, barely twenty-two, who had already been under contract with a major opera house for a year or so, singing leading roles. She was an attractive girl with a lovely lyric voice. One day she wrote, to my horror, that she had been assigned the part of Salome. I acted in a way that **was not** considered cricket in operatic circles. I wrote to the

Lilli Lehmann

Yarmila Novotua

Chaliapin

Battistini

Professor Fuchs as he is today

Intendant of the opera house. I said I could well understand that he wanted a graceful girl for Salome instead of a mature woman of mature dimensions, but he might spoil the entire future of a gifted singer, for the role was intended for a mature and experienced voice. The result was very gratifying. He replied that my arguments had convinced him and that she would not sing Salome. He also wrote to the girl to congratulate her on having a teacher who looked after the best interests of his pupils so energetically.

The third case concerns a friend of mind, conductor at a prominent opera school, who years ago invited me to a performance of *Eugene Onegin*. He wanted me to hear a sensational young singer who was appearing as Tatiana. 'Isn't she wonderful!' he said with pride after the performance. 'The incredible thing is that she's not yet eighteen.' 'Poor girl' I said, 'she is certainly excellent, but I doubt if she will ever make the grade. She will become one of the many frustrated women whose early stage successes prevent them from having an operatic career.' My friend laughed at my Cassandra-like prophecies. But after a few more 'Pyrrhic victories' the girl vanished into oblivion. Many years later she visited me and broke down weeping. She said she had spent her life regretting that she had taken no notice of my warning. For to return to the title of this chapter, Lyric or Dramatic is not the question. It is a false idea—almost a superstition—that progressing from lyric to dramatic means promotion. The point is how to make music fit the capacities of the voice. In singing, as in many things in life, it is the quality that counts.

FROM BARITONE TO
HEROIC TENOR
(MEZZO-SOPRANO TO
SOPRANO[1])

It is one thing to advise a baritone to become a heroic tenor; it is quite another to train him to make the change.

[1] N.B. The advice in this chapter is equally applicable to the mezzo-soprano or contralto who wants to turn soprano. Mezzo-sopranos and contraltos are often taken this

10

In many respects an opera reformer, Richard Wagner created the 'Wagnerian' tenor.[1] But even before his day there were so-called 'Heroic' tenors. Auber, Meyerbeer and Halevy wrote parts in *La Muette de Portici, Robert le Diable, Le Prophet* and *La Juive* which were brilliantly sung by the leading tenors of the Paris Grand Opera, Nourrit, Duprez and Roger. But they were really lyric-dramatic roles demanding endurance, strong personality, and a wide range up to top C. They emphasised the higher part of the range, the part which suits tenors best.

Wagnerian Tenors and Sopranos

For Wagnerian parts the story is different. The tenor has to sing for long stretches of time in a range that is better for a baritone. For his effects Wagner never asks anything higher than an A. Lohengrin, Tannhäuser and Tristan never go beyond A. Stolzing and Siegfried have each one B flat. In *Götterdämmerung*, Siegfried is meant to reach high C, but he may ignore it if he wishes.

The lowest tenor range ever written, and hence the most problematical part, is Siegmund in *Die Walküre*. A only occurs once and the entire range is so low that in spots it is difficult even for a baritone. The middle and lower register of a Wagnerian tenor should always have the characteristic qualities of a baritone, just as a Wagnerian soprano should have the richness and fullness of a mezzo-soprano. Another characteristic common to both is that as a rule they develop later than their lyrical counterparts, just as certain plants take longer to flower than others. That is

---

way if they are young, attractive and talented: they tire of waiting to sing Carmen and Amneris, Eboli or Delilah, all of which require vocal and physical attributes. Many mezzo parts characterise older women, or are secondary roles such as Susuki or Maddalena (*Rigoletto*). But many Rossini roles such as Cenerentola and Rosina have recently come back into vogue in their original versions, and offer a visual and vocal challenge to the mezzo-soprano who masters them.

[1] Seemingly destined to die out, even in Germany.

why a future heroic tenor, who begins to study at seventeen or so, will show all the signs of a baritone and often be taken as one by experienced teachers. The future Brünnhilde or Isolde may at first be classified as a mezzo-soprano or even a contralto. But female Wagnerian singers often have a workable head register from the very beginning, in addition to a rich middle register. With male voices this is less frequent. Sometimes a heroic tenor reaches the opera stage as a baritone before he is recognised as a tenor (see cases cited at the end of this chapter).

The Decision to Change

It is sometimes difficult to decide whether a young baritone is in the process of becoming a heroic tenor or whether he is just a baritone with an exceptionally high range. It is a grave responsibility for a teacher to teach a young baritone a tenor part. That he can often sing a B flat or even an occasional high C is no proof that he could or should study to become a tenor. Opera apart, situations often occur (e.g. in light opera, as cantors in synagogues etc.) in which it is difficult to decide whether a singer is a high baritone or a 'short' tenor. Such singers would run into difficulties if they attempted to sing as real tenors for any length of time.

A teacher should not make a final decision before making a series of tests. Both student and teacher must realise that failure may damage the voice much more than success could enhance it. The road back is hard and dangerous as the change-over often causes damage which may not show itself straight away.

Only rarely does a *lyric* baritone develop into a lyric tenor (see below, Julius Lieban), because the latter requires greater facility as well as a higher range. A heroic tenor on the other hand needs a great deal of volume and resonance to produce the characteristic sound of the Wagnerian tenor. The length of the operas and the size of the orchestra also requires uncommon stamina. Many are beguiled because their appearance is right for these parts, others fall in love with the music. Promising careers have failed from such misplaced devotion.

Making the Change

The next big question is does the singer have the time and patience to see it through? It is difficult to know how long re-training will take, and ample time is essential. Along with the change in technique goes a subtle psychological change. Every baritone has a certain sensation associated with a high F, and it is different from what a tenor feels, since for him F is merely a transition to his higher notes.

General Essentials: It is difficult to lay down rules about re-training. In many years of teaching, I have been able to carry it out four times in all, in each case successfully. I let myself be guided by the following principles, which also apply to mezzo-sopranos who wish to become dramatic sopranos. In concentrated form these principles echo what is found elsewhere in this book:

1. The student must only sing what is recommended by his teacher and avoid anything that reminds him of his baritone past. It is better to stop singing altogether, and certainly to avoid dramatic singing.

2. The middle range has to become the basis of the 'new' voice without sacrificing the distinctive characteristics of the singer.

3. Check for a negative reaction in the middle range after singing in a higher range, and discover the reason for any loss of mellowness or facility.

4. Head resonance is essential. Exercises using the higher range should be given only when head resonance is assured, and should be sung at first in mezza voce. Only when top C can be reached in mezza voce should G, A flat and A be sung in *forte*.

5. The singer should avoid singing a high note which has not first been sung with ease in exercises. Naturally this holds good for any singer, but it is particularly relevant here: do not sing a phrase with your highest note in it, and certainly never in public.

6. When beginning to study tenor roles, the singer should avoid those in a low range which could remind him of his previous career, e.g., Parsifal or Siegmund.

Such retraining resembles a medical cure, only to be undertaken if the singer is prepared to obey instructions implicitly.

Famous Change-overs

In Wagner's time many baritones attempted the change-over without sufficient preparation, e.g. Schnorr von Carolsfeld, the first Tristan, Ferdinand Jaeger (an early Parsifal), and Heinrich Vogel. The second generation of Wagnerian tenors also included many former baritones, the best-known being Eloe Silva. Erik Schmedes, for twenty years a leading Wagnerian tenor at the Vienna opera, Alois Burgstaller, Rudolf Berger and Julius Lieban were other famous cases. Lieban was a fine lyric baritone who became a splendid David (*Meistersinger*) and Mime (*Siegfried*). The change-over was also practised before Wagner's time: one such case was the English tenor John Sims Reeves, who made his debut in the bass part of Count Rodolfo in *Sonambula,* and Enrico Tamberlik, who became an important tenor. Most celebrated of all were Jean de Reszke and Lauritz Melchior.

Jean de Reszke: Clara Leiser in her biography considers it the fault of his first teacher Ciaffai that de Reszke was trained as a baritone. He was only fifteen when he began taking lessons: Ciaffai then recommended him to the well-known baritone Cotogni, with whom he studied for five years, accompanying him on his tours. As every singer unconsciously imitates his teacher it is a small wonder that both teacher and pupil were sure de Reszke was a baritone. So he was at this time: not only did he sing parts, arias and exercises as a baritone, but he had a baritone's psychological approach.

However, at his debut as Alfonso in *La Favorita* at the Teatro Fenice, Venice, a critic commented that his voice had tenor qualities, and he sang an impressive high A at the end of his aria. In London he sang the baritone parts in *Les Huguenots*, *Le Nozze di Figaro* and *Don Giovanni*—all with success. In Paris he made his debut in a buffo bass part, Fra Melitone in *Forza del Destino!*

He decided to change over after a performance as Figaro in *Barbiere*, urged on by colleagues and friends and by his brother Edouard, who had meantime become a famous bass in Paris. Three years later he made his tenor debut as Robert le Diable in Meyerbeer's opera. Then at Massenet's special request he created the tenor role in *Herodias*. From then on it was clear that not only was he a tenor, but one of the greatest the world has seen. He must also have been marvellous in his former career: Bernard Shaw writes that he never heard a better baritone than Jean de Reszke.

Lauritz Melchior: sang as a baritone for eight years at the Royal Opera House in Copenhagen. He made his debut as Silvio in *Pagliacci*, and sang countless baritone parts, including Faninal in *Rosenkavalier*, Wolfram in *Tannhäuser*, and Onegin. As Conte di Luna (*Trovatore*) he interpolated a high C in a performance in which Mme. Cahier was a guest as Azucena and this well-known contralto succeeded in persuading him to re-train his voice. He was given a year's paid leave of absence and studied every day with Wilhelm Herold, an excellent tenor at the Copenhagen Opera. He made a great success of his tenor debut in the formidable role of Tannhäuser. After two more years in Denmark (appearing in *Le Prophet* and other heroic roles, and even in some of his old baritone roles) he went to Germany and Bayreuth and the Metropolitan, where he remained for 24 years.

As the prototype of the Wagnerian tenor, his is an exceptional case, but it shows how a fine voice can develop into a great heroic tenor even after many years as a baritone, and still retain its quality. Of course in this type of retraining one only hears of the successes and not of the failures. For every barrow-boy who rises to fame and fortune there are many who fall anonymously by the wayside.

CHAPTER 8

MUSICAL EDUCATION

Pᴀʀᴀᴅᴏxɪᴄᴀʟ as it may sound, the younger and less experienced the singer, the more he needs a sound musical education. Naturally a good musical background helps a well-established artist, but it is doubly rewarding for a beginner. A novice never gets the same amount of rehearsal time as a star performer; the understudy has to be available at short notice, often without rehearsal. The 'big break' invariably arrives unheralded with scant time for preparation. How many great careers in opera and oratorio have begun as the result of having had the courage and musicianship to take over a part at short notice?

Equally paradoxically, it is dangerous for young singers to be *too* musical, as they may be persuaded to sing something which is not good for their voices: versatility is fraught with danger. Conductors often provide openings (especially in modern music) —but overrate what a young singer can do.

The Musical Education of Singers in the Past

The requirements of opera singing have changed so enormously that the education of present-day singers is bound to be different from what it used to be. Little is known about the education of singers in the period of *bel canto,* but it is clear that they were given complete tuition in all relevant musical subjects. (Monteverdi himself took charge of the vocal and musical preparation of the girl he chose to sing Arianna.) Up to the time of Rossini and even later, opera singers studied harmony and one or more instruments. Giovenale Sacchi (1726-1789) and Charles Burney (1726-1814) both claimed that Farinelli mastered several instruments, including harpsichord, viola d'amore and the mandolin. Opera singers regularly composed their own cadenzas, and some even inserted their own *aria da capo*.[1] Many composers were singers and teachers, e.g. Giulio Caccini (1516-1618) who in 1601 published the epoch-making *Nuove musiche*, Alessandro Stradella (1645-1681), and Francesco Pistocchi (1659-1726), who was the composer-founder of the famous singing school at Bologna, etc.

Stendhal emphasised the influence of Rossini in bringing excessive 'composition' to an end amongst singers, but it was Verdi in his last period who finally put an end to their autocracy. From *Ballo in Maschera* (1859) onwards, they were no longer permitted to insert their own cadenzas and embellishments. Verdi

---

[1] In his *Life of Rossini* (1824), Stendhal tells how Velutti always prepared three different sets of ornamentation for any given passage, and decided according to the mood of the moment which he was going to sing. He narrates an interesting incident (p. 329 of the translated edition by Richard N. Coe, published in U.K. by John Calder in 1956):

'It was in the year 1814 that Rossini journeyed to Milan to work on his opera *Aureliano in Palmira*, and there he met Velutti, who was to have a part in the coming production . . .

'At the first rehearsal with the orchestra, Velutti sang the *aria* straight through, and Rossini was dazzled with admiration; at the second rehearsal, Velutti began to embroider (*fiorire*) the melody, and Rossini, finding the result both exquisite in performance and well in keeping with his own intentions as composer, approved; but at the third rehearsal, the original pattern of the melody had almost entirely *disappeared* beneath a marvellous filigree-work of embroidery and arabesque. At last there dawned the great day of the *première*: . . . a *furore*; but Rossini found himself confronted with insuperable difficulties in trying to identify what Velutti was supposed to be singing; his own music, in fact, had grown completely unrecognisable. For all that, however, Velutti's performance was a thing of unparalleled beauty, and enjoyed untold popularity with the audience, which, after all, can never be blamed for applauding something which it so wholeheartedly enjoys.'

Velutti was once made fun of by sixteen-year-old Maria Garcia, later Maria Malibran. In 1827 she had a last-minute chance of taking over a leading part in Zingarelli's opera *Romeo e Giulietta*, at the King's Theatre, London. Her partner Velutti won tremendous applause for 'embroidering' an aria. The young debutante then repeated his *fioriture* and even added to his *colorature*. The audience applauded her roundly, but Velutti was furious and whispered '*Bricconal*' (rascal).

once conducted a rehearsal of *Ballo* in which Battistini was singing Renato. Battistini interpolated a high note, as he would do in Bellini or Donizetti. Verdi interrupted the rehearsal: 'Signor Battistini, I am the composer, you are the singer.'

The Musical Education of Present-day Singers

Verdi wrote a letter in 1871 about reforming the curriculum of music study. 'I would wish,' he said, 'a comprehensive knowledge in music, exercises in note attack, a very long study of solfeggi as in past time.' This is still valid. A serious student of singing should have an all-round musical education, and take piano lessons. It is always a help if he plays a stringed instrument. A violinist has to check the intonation of every note, form intervals correctly, and link notes in a smooth sequence. What is more, he has to tune the instrument himself. The only danger is that the jaw tends to stiffen because a player has constantly to press on the instrument with the muscles of neck and jaw. My advice is to study cello, in which the player has the same note-by-note discipline without risking the jaw. There have, of course, been notable exceptions. Marcella Sembrich, for instance, was a violin virtuoso before becoming one of the best coloratura sopranos of her time.

Learning conducting is also an excellent discipline. It is a kind of prompting, and a conductor will always appreciate a singer who understands his silent language. A student anxious to sing opera and oratorio should learn to 'conduct' entire scores from start to finish. Following a score in this way is much better than marking time with the feet, clapping, etc., which are subject to unconscious mistakes of rhythm. He should adopt the standard method of all conductors, marking each accent by a downbeat. There are plenty of good handbooks available.

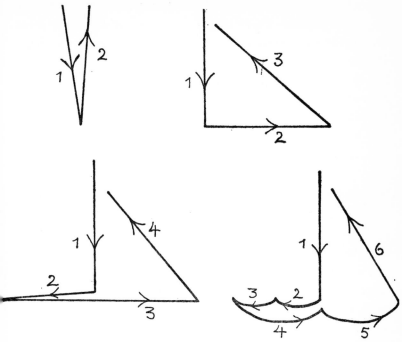

2 in a bar, 3 in a bar, 4 in a bar, 6 in a bar.

The necessity of studying from a piano score, in which the orchestral parts are condensed into two lines, is very misleading, a look into an orchestral partitur will teach him that even when a singer has a leading role, it only appears as a single line in the score, and he has to learn to regard himself as one more element under the conductor's guidance. His own musicianship is all the more essential in that he performs from memory, and has to act at the same time.

A singer's need to study acting has no parallel in other branches of music study. He should never make his first appearance on stage in anything too difficult, or sing anything requiring too much concentration (e.g. no high notes!). The simpler the role,

the better. I am much in favour of letting students begin with
Bastien e Bastienne, the charming opera Mozart wrote at twelve
for Dr. Messmer's private garden theatre in Vienna.[1] Students
learn to move in keeping with the character of the part, and to
feel the rhythm of the music. Already as a child Mozart had an
astonishing feeling for the stage, and his music always characterises
the dramatic action. There are many other little operas which are
highly suitable for students. I have adapted a few one-act operas
by Offenbach as good training material.

Singers versus modern music ?[2]

'Modern music' is a relative term. In the past many compositions have been dubbed 'modern' which to a later generation are
antiquated. Many singers are hostile to modern music, others
like it but refuse to sing it. Many conductors and musicians disagree with this point of view. They forget that in tackling
modern music, a singer jeopardises his tone and his legato. The
quality or durability of an instrument is not affected by what is
performed, be it Bach, Gershwin or a twelve-note composer: but
singers with too much modern music in their repertoire will not
sing as long as Patti or Battistini. A singer has to know what is
good for his voice, and what he has to avoid. That Mr. X or Miss
Z sang modern music for many years without coming to any
harm means that they were more resilient than the average singer.

I once accepted as a student a woman who was already a well-
known concert-singer, and had specialised in modern songs. She
'created' many of them, and the composers frequently accompanied her. She was rightly admired for her intelligence, musicality and application. Her manager, however, wanted to get

---

[1] A favourite teaching choice of the great Wagnerian singer, Anna von Mildenburg.

[2] I realise I may be suspect as an enemy of modern music, but that is not the case. I
sang such songs in my concerts, many for the first time, and was fortunate enough to
study with the late Erwin Stein, champion of Schönberg, Berg, Webern and Britten. As a
responsible teacher, however, I must point out the dangers.

her a contract as an opera singer, and realised that she was not in a condition to tackle the usual repertoire. I made it a condition of acceptance that she abandon all singing for six months, and work on 'tuning' the voice, i.e., an intensive study of legato. She then made a successful debut in a Mozart opera, which satisfied everybody. Many confessed that previously they had never liked her voice, only her excellent rendering of interesting songs.

The gulf between singers and modern music needs examining from both sides. Much is written uncomfortably for the voice, either wilfully or in ignorance of the laws of singing. If his music does not suit singers, the composer has, of course, to accept his fate. Singers who can attract large audiences may refuse to spend time and effort on an unrewarding task, and it will be entrusted to vocally less distinguished performers. The insensitiveness of some composers to the nature and limits of the voice is apt to be a boomerang which hurts their own compositions. If only they would learn about voices! They should learn to sing themselves, regardless of whether their voice is good or bad. As a child prodigy Mozart frequently heard one of the finest singers of the day, the castrato Manzuoli, and probably studied with him as well. Haydn worked for a time as accompanist to Porpora, and Salieri gave some shrewd advice to the young Meyerbeer in Vienna: 'Go to Italy, and learn how to write for the voice.' Today, of course, there are electronic, atonal and 'serial' composers in Italy too—but they keep their sensitivity to vocal sound. The more a composer understands an instrument, the better will he compose for it. Many would indeed have been forgotten had they not possessed a knack of writing for some instrument: Max Bruch, Wieniawsky, Sarasate have all written violin music which virtuosi love to play, and audiences to hear. Lieder will be sung as long as audiences enjoy concerts, not only because they are masterpieces, but because they give the singer so much chance to sing them well. Audiences will never tire of Shakespeare's plays, nor actors of playing them, because they are written (to quote Otto Ludwig) 'out of the heart of actors.'

It is no mere chance that of the many songs a well-known composer may write, the same ones are heard over and over again. Of Schubert's six hundred Lieder, only a hundred are constantly heard. As a young singer, I sang three of Richard Strauss' songs. When I told him I was going to include many unknown ones in a recital of his music, he said: 'We have to face the fact that some songs will be sung again and again, whilst many which we think good are ignored. When this happens, there is always a reason. Either they don't give the singer enough opportunity, or else the music or the poem is not so inspired. Think about your success first, young man: do the ones which show off your voice and your artistry—and avoid experiments.'

CHAPTER 9

MUSICAL AND DRAMATIC EXPRESSION

THE MYTH OF BEL CANTO

Bel canto is used to describe a period, the golden age of singing. It is also a *style* of singing derived from the music of the period, which is taken as a barely attainable ideal for many later styles of singing (e.g. Wagner, veristic opera of Mascagni, Puccini, etc.) where the dramatic declamation presents it with a formidable challenge.

It means just what it says, 'beautiful singing' and it is difficult to trace the origin of the term. It is the art of singing according to the old Italian method of the 17th and 18th centuries, as opposed to the dramatic style of later periods. *It is the art of making music with the voice as an end in itself.* All voices habitually cultivated the art of embellishment (*fioriture,* cadenzas, scales, trills, ornaments) and a very pure, concentrated sound in legato.

It only began to be a slogan when the voice came into competition with the orchestra, and the art of controlled singing began to be restricted to the music which had given rise to it. Nowadays it is used and abused as a trade-mark in teachers' advertisements, although it is doubtful whether anyone who uses the term for publicity would be able to guide students to a way of singing which genuinely deserves this description.

To an unimaginable extent, the art depended on long undisturbed periods of regular study with no outer distraction—nowadays the hardest condition to obtain. Mancini relates how his teacher, the renowned Bernacchi (1685–1756) came to study with one of the masters of the old Italian school:

'One of Pistocchi's most famous pupils was Antonio Bernacchi of Bologna. He himself confessed that he was not gifted with a good voice. He was persuaded by his friends, and decided to trust himself completely to Pistocchi's guidance, who greeted him kindly and at once mapped out for him a study plan to remove his defects and help him to derive benefit from continuous application. Bernacchi courageously undertook the task, and was prepared to study for as long as his teacher required. He never missed his daily lesson, so as to avail himself of his teacher's advice. During the time of study, he not only refused to sing in any churches and theatres, but even for his most intimate friends. He continued to do this until he was given permission to do otherwise. Then he startled the world with his art.'

It sounds like a fairy tale, starting 'Once upon a time . . .'

It is noteworthy that *bel canto* has been considered to be in decline for some while. In 1723 Pier Francesco Tosi (1647–1727) uttered a warning in his classic work *Opinioni de' cantori antichi e moderni*:[1]

'Keep a close watch on two singers of the fair sex who with differing strength are preventing the already declining art from completely decaying' . . . one (Francesca Cuzzoni) has a touching and heartwarming delivery, the other (Faustini Bordoni) has astonishing agility, an unrivalled executive skill and virtuosity. Cuzzoni has a ravishing *cantabile* and sweetness of sound together with pure intonation, perfectly chosen embellishments and assur-

---

[1] According to Handel's biographer, Mainwaring, one 'angelic creature' (Cuzzoni) had a heated argument with Handel before her debut in his London operatic season. She refused to sing the aria *Falsa immagine* from *Ottone*, so the gigantic Handel grabbed hold of her and held her out of an open window, which quickly made her change her mind. Cuzzoni and Bordoni were the famous rivals of Handel's London company; they were protected by factions of London society. When they appeared together on stage in 1727 for Bononcini's opera *Astyanax*, the audience split up and began to urge on their favourite. The two primadonnas flew into a passion, thrashed each other, tore off each other's wig and dress, assisted by the gallery throng. The theatre was at once closed. Their mastery of *bel canto* did not restrain these divas from deplorable excess . . . Faustina Bordoni later married the opera composer, Johann Adolph Hasse, and was for many years one of the most famous singers of her day; Francesca Cuzzoni enjoyed several years of great success, and then died in poverty, as a worker in an Italian button factory.

ance in interpretation. What a priceless mixture would result if these two angelic creatures were to combine in a single person!'

There is much to suggest that *bel canto* was always fighting a losing battle. In 1777, for instance, Giambattista Mancini wrote in his *Practical Reflections on the Art of Singing* (at this time he was singing master at the Viennese Imperial Court):

'It may puzzle my readers that, although there are many great Italian artists flourishing all over the world, the idea has taken root in Italy, and abroad as well, that our vocal art is in decline, and that we lack fitting schools and good singers.'

With surprising modernity, he blames the decline on to teachers who have not learnt the rules and who offer their services for less than a good teacher can afford, finding students who are attracted by the idea of economy.

One reason for the decline of *bel canto* was the development of the opera orchestra. The court organist and composer, Heinrich Gerber (1702–1775), who had studied with J. S. Bach, wrote that

'Since 1740 it is impossible to understand the words of opera singers, because the orchestra drowns their voices. The extravagance of the orchestra is now in general vogue.'

Advocates of *bel canto* such as Johann Adolph Hasse (1699–1783), Niccolo Jomelli (1714–1774) and G. P. Telemann (1681–1767) repeatedly warned that the orchestra was jeopardising the singers' voices; even in church music the 'theatrical style' of orchestral writing was rapidly displacing the contrapuntal style. Mozart wrote from Paris in 1778:

'and then the singers . . . one can't even call these people singers . . . for they don't sing, they yell . . . from their throats . . . from their noses . . .'

In 1818 a critic wrote in the Viennese *Music Magazine*:

'Although there are many outstanding instrumental artists, the art of singing is certainly declining. The success of *Tancredi* by the twenty-one-year-old Rossini expresses the pleasure of the audience in hearing the real *bel canto* once again.'

At the first performance of Meyerbeer's *Le Prophete* in 1849, Franz Liszt described Viardot-Garcia (for whom the part of Fides was written) as 'the uncontested mistress of the lost art of singing'.

In the middle of the century, after the première of *Ballo in Maschera* in 1859, Verdi wrote to the impresario:

'You must admit I am a model of self-abnegation for not vanishing with the score under my arm to search for dogs who would bark less than the singers who were cast for my opera . . .'

When Eduard Hanslik visited Rossini in Paris in 1860, Rossini confessed that he had not been to an opera for sixteen years:

'It is that they have long since ceased to sing. Now they yell and bark, and box . . .'

Three years later he accepted twenty-four vocalisers dedicated to him by Mathilde Marchesi (1821–1913) and he wrote in his letter:

'. . . please be faithful to your task of teaching the real Italian tradition. It excludes neither expression nor dramatic power, but nowadays this is simply becoming a matter of the lungs, without study . . .'

Another important reason for the decline of *bel canto* was the disappearance of the *castrati*, who represented the perfect vehicle for an art which was built round exquisite vocal sounds and long breaths. Opera had become a singer's art soon after the first *dramma in musica* in Florence in 1594. Alessandro Scarlatti (1659–1725) in 115 operas and Handel (1685–1759) in 46, for instance, gave singers the chance to excel. There were a few outstanding women singers, but the protagonists were generally virtuoso *castrati*, who with a man's size and strength produced female sound, and rarified and embellished it with all the artistic single-mindedness of abnormally specialised human beings. Gluck (1714–1787) was the first to challenge their uncontested supremacy. In the introduction to *Alceste* (Vienna, 1767) he writes:

'When I undertook to write the music for *Alceste*, I resolved to divest it of all the abuses introduced into Italian opera either by the mistaken vanity of singers or the great complacency of composers, which have so long made the most splendid and beautiful of spectacles into the most ridiculous and wearisome. I have tried to make the music express the poetry and follow the situations of the story, without interrupting the action or stifling it with a useless superfluity of ornaments . . .' It was a complete novelty in that period for all the male parts to be sung by men, and not by *castrati*. For the first time basses were used in heroic operas, as up to then they had only appeared in buffo (comic) parts.

In *Orpheus* (Vienna, 1762) Gluck had written the leading part for an alto *castrato*, Guardagni; but when he performed it in Paris in 1774 he rewrote the part for a tenor (Legros). *Castrati* were never fashionable in France as they were in Italy (their country of origin) and in England, Germany, Russia, etc.

Mozart (1756–1791) developed Italian opera and founded the German at the same time. In his youth, he had to deliver hand-tailored arias to the *castrati* who sang in the operas he composed for the Italian *stagioni*, but in *Idomeneo* (Munich, 1781) he wrote the title role for the tenor Raaf, and the second part for the *castrato* Del Prato. This was his last association with a castrato. In subsequent operas he introduced more realistic human beings taken from the life of the time: *Nozze di Figaro* was not only a milestone in the development of opera, but also for the development of singers.

Bel Canto[1] in Italy had three important champions after Mozart: Gioacchino Rossini (1792–1868), the last representative of the florid singing style: Vincenzo Bellini (1801–1835), the elegiac

[1] Mattia Battistini (1857–1928) is often described as the last belcantist; although he never heard these great singers (he made his debut in 1878 with *La Favorita* at the Teatro Argentina, Rome), his teacher was known to all the great artists of that epoch. Battistini excelled in the operas of Bellini and Donizetti, and liked to add his own embellishments.

composer who wrote so melodically for singers, and Gaetano Donizetti (1797–1848), who composed sixty-three romantic operas, most of them immensely successful. Bellini was lucky to find an unsurpassed quintet of excellent artists for his ten operas: Giulia Grisi, the tenor, Rubini, the baritone, Tamburini, and the famous bass Lablache, not to mention Giuditta Pasta, who created Norma and the title-role of *Somnambula*. This period could be called the *neo bel canto* period, and the earlier one is often forgotten in its favour. Rossini was already beginning to champ against the excessive liberties taken by singers. Henri Beyle (Stendhal) relates how he was outraged by the autocratic habits of the castrato Giovanni Battista Velluti (1781–1861), and insisted that singers should only sing cadenzas and embellishments he himself had composed.

Verdi did not cease to write melodiously for his singers, but by 1859 he did not allow them to sing their own embellishments, and asked more of them emotionally and dramatically. Wagner's attitude to bel canto is curiously in opposition to the challenge he brought to it. In his early years as an operatic conductor and composer, he explicitly favoured it:

'Why can't we Germans admit openly and freely', he wrote while he was a conductor at Magdeburg, 'that the Italian is superior to the German in song?' and '. . . without perfect vocal technique, the highest kind of expression is impossible.' Like Verdi, he was enchanted by the

'limpid melody, the simple, noble, lovely song of Bellini . . . it is surely not a sin to confess this and believe in it; perhaps it would not even be a sin if, before we went to sleep, we were to pray that some day German composers might achieve such melodies and such art of handling song. *Gesang,* and *Gesang,* ye Germans!'[1]

---

[1] As translated by Ernest Newman in *Wagner as Man and Artist*. Newman adopts the word for song, but Wagner clearly had *bel canto* in mind.

Even his later works can be sung by well-trained *bel canto* singers according to the principles of *bel canto*, as those who heard Lilly Lehmann's Brünnhilde and Isolde, or Jean de Reszke's Tristan will readily testify. A later generation can listen to the love duet of *Tristan* sung by Frida Leider or by Kerstin Flagstad in recordings, with Melchior as Tristan. Yet many Wagnerian singers, as W. J. Henderson describes in *The Art of Singing*

'bark, cough or sneeze the notes, instead of producing them in a normal manner'.

The third generation was much more competent: they often sang in operas by Verdi, Meyerbeer, etc., and took pains to produce more legato singing combined with the necessary dramatic accentuation.

France was the third great nation whose composers were influenced by her singers, and vice versa. Her *grande opéra* came through foreigners (Gluck, Cherubini, Spontini, Meyerbeer and Rossini) and was given native expression by Auber (1782–1871) and Halévey (1799–1862), and later by Gounod (1818–1893), Massenet (1842–1912) and Bizet (1838–1875). Within a single decade, two outstanding tenors, Adolpe Nourrit (1802–1875) and Gilbert Duprez (1806–1896) created a new, immensely strenuous, but very effective type: the French dramatic tenor. *Bel canto* was still prevalent, but the dramatic demands of this music were enormous. Jean de Reszke (1850–1925) was the last great exponent of the period, which included famous basses such as Nicholas Levasseur (1791–1871) and Baritones J. Baptiste Fauré (1830–1914) and Jean Lasalle (1847–1914), not to mention Jean de Reszke's bass brother Edouard (1855–1917) and the bass Pol Plançon (1848–1914).

In the meantime, as categories of voices, high coloratura sopranos and, to a lesser extent, high lyric tenors retain the last vestiges of a legendary art. It is perhaps comforting to think that even the long-winded, long-studied and undistracted *castrati* would not have found Zerbinetta's *coloratura* in *Ariadne auf Naxos* pure child's play!

HOW DO PRESENT-DAY SINGERS COMPARE WITH THEIR PREDECESSORS?

Were the singers of the past better than present-day singers? Nobody can really answer that question, as there is nobody alive today who heard Jenny Lind, Giovanni Battista Rubini, or their colleagues, and old records of more recent artists only give a shadow of the truth, though they often indicate a musical standard much more easy-going than our own.

Clearly, singers who for years sing strenuous parts in differing types of opera, especially in Wagner, Strauss or contemporary music, cannot be compared for sheer beauty of sound with artists who only sang and spoke their native language (Italian), and never sang a note which was contrary to the principles of 'beautiful singing'.

But let us not be unfair. How big was the repertoire of the 'matadors' compared with that of modern singers? None of them would force himself to sing anything that did not exactly fit his voice and his way of singing. The composer had to suit the singer, not vice versa. Before writing an aria for a singer, the young Mozart would familiarise himself with his particular type of voice and talent. If a singer sang in ensemble, he would only do what he was accustomed to doing. The conductor was the more or less devoted accompanist. A singer did not have to ride a symphony orchestra at least 100 strong, four or five times larger than the orchestra used by Handel and his contemporaries, tuned a semi-tone higher (if not more). Nor did he have to tire himself out in long rehearsals, and be bothered by the demands of the pro-ducer in an age which judges a performance primarily with its eyes. Luisa Tetrazzini reflects the belcantist outlook on rehearsal when she writes in her book *How to Sing*[1]:

[1] Published by C. A. Pearson, London, 1923.

'Rehearsals are a necessary evil, and the sensible artist will try to make the best of them. Undoubtedly they are very tedious and trying, but they are quite unavoidable, unless you happen to have obtained sufficient eminence to dispense with them. Even then it is not always wise to avoid them if you wish to produce the best results.

'Patti, throughout the greater part of her career, never attended any rehearsals. But then she always sang in the best-known operas with thoroughly experienced fellow artists, who were carefully instructed as to her requirements. It is hardly necessary to say that her case was exceptional.'

With the rise of Verdi in Italy and Wagner in Germany, the absolute reign of the opera singer began to shake, and the composer began to dictate. He was displaced by the conductor, who now has to struggle[1] against the rising dictatorship of the producer with his powerfully-equipped assistants, the set and costume designer and the lighting technician. The job of producing used to be a semi-retirement for *bassi-buffi* who were glad not to be bothered too much (the producer is still very subordinate in Italy, except in major productions). A producer can disturb an opera more than a singing star, who can only be seen and heard during their own particular performance. An invisible producer can draw attention to himself throughout an opera by abandoning traditional staging in favour of something 'new'. Opera producers need to be musical, and many of them are in fact trained musicians. The danger comes from straight stage producers who think they can make opera more interesting by teaching opera singers to be perfect actors. How different from the days of the *castrati,* when Senesino, at Farinelli's debut in Hasse's *Artaserse* in London in 1734, could break out of his part as a 'pitiless tyrant' to embrace the 'prisoner', because of his beautiful singing!

---

[1] Hence the number of well-known conductors (Karajan, Klemperer, etc.) who prefer to do their own staging.

In the name of modern stage discipline the modern opera singer has to swallow all manner of extravaganzas and excel in feats of memory never dreamt of by his predecessors. He has to tackle in rapid alternation a series of parts dissimilar in style, language and range, and face critics who care much less about a well-trained voice than about a correct style for each opera. Operatic schedules of even 100 years ago were filled with operas which in structure and technical requirements were very similar. Rossini once jokingly remarked: 'When you know one of my operas, you know all of them.' Think by contrast of the repertoire of a modern opera house!

Our own generation has developed astonishing skill in learning musically difficult parts. A hundred years ago leading singers of the Vienna Court Opera rehearsed *Tristan und Isolde* for several months, but had to abandon the idea of performance because of 'unsurmountable musical difficulties'. Eduard Hanslik writes in his *Musikalisches Skizzenbuch* that Wagner's personally chosen first Tristan, Alois Ander, said to him: 'We know the second act from memory already, but in the meantime we've forgotten the first!'

And then the hectic intercontinental travelling schedules and the hazards and swift adaptations they impose. At the beginning of the century artists would appear every third day before an audience, and Battistini was considered exceptional as he was able to sing every second day. Today rehearsal and performance may take place in the same half of the day, and within a week a singer can appear not only in three cities but in three continents. Compare all this with Farinelli's *tour de force,* employed for ten years at the Spanish Court to minister to the King's melancholia by singing the same four arias night after night. It may have exercised his inventive faculty to the uttermost, but it could not harm his voice.

My devout prayer is that the difficulties facing present-day singers would be considered by the people involved, whether as conductors, producers, managers, critics or audience. The retrogression in the art of singing can only be explained in terms of the circumstances in which we live today. Future singers will probably be replaced by robots! Although there are still teachers who can guide a student to the heights of achievement, the enticements to lure him away from study are too great to be resisted, not to mention the greatly increased competition. Who can blame a gifted but impoverished young singer for accepting a premature offer? Theoretically he should never stop developing his voice, but in practice he has to go ahead and prepare himself for his next job.

A student can only be advised to study as hard as he can for as long as he can. With daily practice a singer can constantly improve his tone and obtain a smoother and more relaxed legato. There are certainly great singers today, singing under far more difficult conditions than their predecessors, but never ceasing to improve voice and technique. Patti once said:

'We artists will still be learning when we are too old to sing.'

RECITATIVE AND SPRECHGESANG

Although recitatives were used in pre-operatic church music, they only began to develop after the first opera, *Dafne,* was composed by Jacopo Peri in 1597 to a libretto by Rinuccini. In an aria, music is the most important element, whilst in recitative the natural articulation of the words and their meaning takes first place. Accompanied recitative is used in *opera seria,* and *secco* recitative in *opera buffa.* The latter used to be accompanied by a harpsichord; nowadays a piano may be used. Accompanied recitative (*recitativo rappresentativo*) is accompanied by the orchestra. In *secco* recitative the singer needs declamatory skill and distinct articulation, as in spoken dialogue. The conductor fixes the tempo for individual phrases in rehearsal, but does not conduct it in performance. *Recitativo rappresentativo*, on the other hand, is conducted like an aria or ensemble.

Opera singers have to master both types. It is, however, inadvisable to start studying recitative too soon, as it is one of the most difficult things for a singer to learn. It is only too easy when singing it to forget the fundamental principles of voice-placement and breath control. An inexpert singer over-emphasises the words and endangers the vocal line; he may abandon the vocal line altogether in *secco* recitative and over-sing a sung recitative, tiring himself out before the following aria has even begun.

Anyone who can teach the art of recitative deserves much gratitude. *Secco* recitative is Italian speech-rhythm set to music, though its technique can be applied to any language. It must be declaimed as melodiously as possible and always absolutely in tune. Good Italian singers can do it for long stretches, as can be heard in recordings of Italian operas. A well-trained singer can even warm up his voice on recitative. Battistini's command of it was extraordinary. I was lucky enough to hear him as Don Giovanni three times in three weeks. When he started the recitative that precedes *La ci darem la mano* I understood why Zerlina was unable to resist him! He had a wonderful flexibility which enabled him to change smoothly from piano and pianissimo to forte and fortissimo.

Spoken dialogue in Italian opera is almost unknown, but is always used in *opéra comique* and *Singspiel*, the original forms of French and German opera, in which sung recitative is never used. *Fidelio, Der Freischütz* and Marschner's *Hans Heiling* all include important scenes in dialogue. Verdi reverted to the original meaning of the word *melodrama* when he departed from normal Italian tradition and had Lady Macbeth reading the letter from her husband exactly as in Shakespeare's play; the orchestra accompanies the spoken words with a sustained chord through four bars. Six years later, in *Traviata*, Violetta also reads a letter, but this time Verdi obtains a most touching effect by accompanying the spoken words with the beautiful melody of Alfredo's first love song, played dolcissimo by violins. In *La Boheme* Rodolfo uses his speaking voice at the end of the opera; whilst Gianni Schicchi addresses the audience in a wittily spoken epilogue.

In Mozart's operas all kinds of styles are found, from typical Italian with traditional recitative to German *Singspiel* with spoken dialogue (e.g. *Bastien and Bastienne*, *Entführung*). *Magic Flute* combines both types, while in *Figaro* and *Don Giovanni* instrumentally accompanied recitative is wonderfully used as though it were the *secco* recitative of opera buffa. Just as Shakespeare used blank verse in dialogue for elevated characters and the more popular dialogue for inferior characters, so the recitativo stromantato is used to perfection in *Figaro* and *Don Giovanni* like the secco recitativo of opera buffa.

The 'Sprechgesang' first used by Richard Wagner is derived from recitative in all its forms. Compare the powerful recitative preceding Donna Anna's aria:

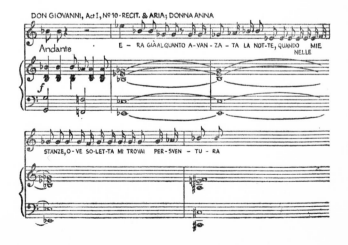

with Telramund's dramatic narration in *Lohengrin*:

The two recitatives are very similar, and even use the same key. Donna Anna's recitative reaches a most effective climax with the outburst:

A direct bridge leads from Mozartian recitative to *Sprechgesang* in Wagner, Strauss and modern composers. Wotan's and Tristan's narrations, for instance, are based on technical principles which a well-equipped singer will already have met in the accompanied recitatives of *opera seria*. On the other hand, many of the phrases of Hans Sachs, Eva, Ochs von Lerchenau and others are closely related to *secco* recitative. Modern operas and operattas can only be mastered when a singer has a thorough grounding in older forms of recitative. In some, e.g., Wozzeck, the composer uses a *Sprechgesang* which is not based on traditional musical rules: the words are dominant as in all recitative, but the method of attacking and sustaining the tone is on the boundary between speaking and singing, and involves perilous leaps. In modern operas generally, recitative is mixed with arioso and dramatic musical phrases.

As modern opera houses **have** a very varied repertoire, two different categories of singer tend to appear—those who handle any part which requires singing, and those who specialise in modern opera. The latter need to be very competent actors. Occasionally first-class artists can handle both types. The category to which any particular student belongs will become clear during his period of study.

Oratorio recitative is different from operatic recitative and must be learnt as a specialised art.[1] In operettas and light operas the artistic demands are not so high, but it is essential to know how to sing recitative as, for instance in Gilbert and Sullivan, the art of pointing couplets is based on it. It is also essential for all art-songs from Schubert to our own day.

INSPIRATION—EMOTION—
EXPRESSION

'For in the very torrent, tempest, and (as I may say) whirlwind of your passion, you must beget a temperance that may give it smoothness.'

HAMLET, Act II, sc. 2.

In so far as he is not a routine craftsman, a painter, composer or poet needs inspiration for the right creative mood, and often needs to wait for it to come. A performing stage artist on the other hand needs to be able to enter a 'recreating mood' at a particular moment. Many singers of course never attempt it. They sing their songs or their part as well as they can, and that is that; they do not excite an audience or communicate strong emotion. Others, through a combination of skill and imagination, transform themselves into the character they are playing. This transformation (or capacity to 'recreate') is essential for such roles

[1] To mention only one important part in Oratoria: The Evangelist in J. S. Bach, passion music needs not only a particular high tenor, but also a certain style for the narration.

as Canio, Salome, Elektra, Otello, Boris Godunov, etc., but singers who can handle these roles for years are definitely in a minority. Victor Maurel (1848–1923), 'creator' of Iago and Falstaff, puts the problem well:

'In the time of the school of bel canto it was not usual for a teacher to discuss expression with students. No one expected expression of true emotions from a singer—the audience only wanted to listen to harmonious notes. In our day the audience wants real emotions. But these are apt to present difficulties in singing, which the student cannot handle.'[1]

The sheer act of singing constantly hampers the act of transformation. An opera singer's actions spring from the music and the conductor's beat, and he cannot be as single-minded in interpretation as an actor. It is interesting to compare Sir John Gielgud's experience with Stanislavsky's practical experience of opera singers:

'. . . everybody was pleased with my ability in the emotional scenes. (A play by Drinkwater, in which he was replacing Claude Rains, quoted in his autobiography). Their feeling came to me without much difficulty, and the sincerity of such feeling 'got over' to the audience, despite my lack of technical accomplishments.'[2]

'How can you hope to pick out the composer's rhythm if you are preoccupied with the fear of making a mistake, or believe your voice sounds a little hoarse? And how can you possibly enter into the life of the composer's rhythm if it is all too clear that you are afraid of the high notes?'

But when technique and emotional intensity work together, an opera singer can achieve even greater effects than an actor.

[1] *Zehn Jahre aus meinem Kuenstlerleben* (1887–1897), translated into German by Lilly Lehmann.
Raabe & Flothow, Berlin, 1899.
[2] Early Stages, Macmillan Press, New York, 1939. By John Gielgud.

Chaliapin's Boris Godunov and Maria Jeritza's Tosca were memorable masterpieces of characterisation. Lilly Lehmann's dramatic effects are unforgettable even at many years' distance: when as Donna Anna she recognised Don Giovanni as her father's murderer, or as Norma tried to kill her sleeping children and stopped at the last moment to embrace them: or as in *Fidelio*, when she answered her husband's moving question 'Oh meine Leonore, was hast du für mich getan?' (O Leonore, what have you done for me?) with the simple words 'Nichts, nichts, mein Florestan' (Nothing, my Florestan). Not many at those performances could keep back their tears.

Learning to Feel a Part

A good singer needs to be able to express both musically and dramatically. The first he has in common with all musicians. The second has its origin in the words and the situation. The second kind is superficially easier to acquire, just as a young actor prefers to play a dramatic scene rather than one with little or no gesture, where the weight of the situation is carried in his words and facial expression. In actual fact dramatic acting requires great subtlety, for 'hamming' can spoil the illusion.

Expression cannot be taught: emotion is not a matter of rules. But a student can learn a great deal from a teacher who constantly sings the same phrases with expression. To quote Maurel again:

'The teacher can overcome them (i.e., the difficulties of expression) if he knows the secret of how to do it in his own singing. Yet a student will often be consoled with this sort of thing "The truth of expression is a matter of artistic emotion. If you feel inspired, you will find it. Otherwise you will hunt for such feeling in vain.'[1]

---

[1] Ibid.

How much emotion a singer expresses in singing depends on how free he feels, and how much he is in control of his emotion, as well as on his capacity for feeling. 'When technical obstacles are removed, a student often finds it easier to show emotion, and expression comes naturally. Some catch fire from others, others remain cold even when they are sharing the stage with emotionally expansive singers. A certain predisposition is needed, and if it is not there, nobody can awaken it. 'Thou canst not speak of that thou dost not feel.'[1] Even in ordinary life, some people speak expressively, while others are quite impassive, whether they talk or listen. It is sad when they have singing talent, because they are often hopeless cases. There is a pleasant story of Sir Henry Irving, who was once rehearsing a young actress in the wooing scene of Richard III. He grew impatient when she showed no emotion, and finally pinched her behind. She yelled. 'That's what I want', he said.

As a beginner on stage, I was eager to sing and act expressively long before I had mastered my voice. This kept me back for a long time. I was never able to sing my operatic roles as well as I sang them in rehearsal, as my feeling ran away with me. Plenty of opportunity to repeat the role gave me the control I needed. Nothing is more valuable to young singers than repeated performances within a few weeks or months (as is possible in German opera houses), though naturally a single performance is better than none at all. It is heartbreaking for a singer to realise after one performance that he could improve if only he were given a chance to work himself deeper into the role. It is a happy coincidence when opera singers have acting talent: generally what happens is that they acquire sufficient stage experience to execute the necessary minimum, or make do with the essential arm movements, like swimmers, in a clumsy effort to satisfy the stage directions!

[1] *Romeo and Juliet*, Act 3, sc. 3.

Many actors can only portray characters that suit their personality. Only a rare talent can develop imagination to its height and acquire the childlike pliability which a real actor needs. Lawrence Olivier and Alec Guinness are notable actors of this type, able to transform themselves from one character to another. A singer needs to express the feeling of the character the composer has in mind, not his own individual reaction to it. I am quite sure I would not spend my time with a chambermaid in an obscure inn if I was engaged to a pretty young girl. But my personal inclinations would have no importance and would have to be submerged. I would acquire the feelings and trappings of Ochs von Lerchenau (*Rosenkavalier*) and immerse myself in the feeling of his period.

At twenty-two Mozart wrote a dramatic scene for insertion in Paisiello's opera *Andromeda* (*Ah, los previdi*, K. 272). He wrote to Aloysia Weber:

'I advise you to watch the expression marks—to think carefully of the meaning and the force of the words—to put yourself in all seriousness into Andromeda's situation and position and to imagine that you really are that very person.'

Jean de Reszke describes the most satisfying experience an interpretative artist can have in a letter to the critic Hermann Klein (31 March 1894) about his portrayal of Werther in French in Chicago:

'In an artist's life, every new role is a stage in a long journey towards the summit of arts, the beautiful and the infinite. The true path—that of emotion—is the goal for which I have been striving all my life. It was reached in the presence of a public which did not understand the words, but which divined by instinct my conception of the character, arising from such simple unexaggerated truth as age and maturity alone can confer on a thinking artist.'

12

'Taste cannot be controlled by law.'

THOMAS JEFFERSON, Notes on Money, 1784.

Is good taste in singing something which can be learnt? The correct answer to that question would have to be yes and no. Good taste can be learnt, but not through books; only by listening to the tasteful singing of others. However, the student must have some understanding of the matter, and sufficient taste to learn from the right models.

Here is an example of what artistry and good taste can mean in singing. Carlo Broschi, called Farinelli, was a famous castrato and probably the most perfect singer the world has ever known. According to his biographer, Giovenale Sachi, Farinelli went to Bologna at twenty-two to compete with the famous castrato Antoni Bernacchi. Farinelli sang first and carried the house with him because of his unusually beautiful voice. Bernacchi's voice was no match for his, but he sang with such art and style that Farinelli admitted defeat. The next morning they left for Rome, where Farinelli became Bernacchi's pupil, and learned the essential quality that he had lacked.

In singing we have to know what kinds of tones and musical phrases are correct in an Italian aria, how to use our voice and vocal technique in a church song. This ability to perform different musical pieces can and must be developed under the guidance of an experienced pedagogue—the subject is called the building of musical style.

Unfortunately, the word 'style' is somewhat misused these days, since in popular singing some characteristics are used which are nothing more than bad habits due to lack of technique.

CHAPTER 10

PROFESSIONAL QUESTIONS

'All of us, when well, give good
advice to the sick.'
TERENCE: Andria, 11, c—160 B.C.
'Never give advice unless asked.'
German proverb.

Some people love giving advice and often know little more than the person they want to advise. It must be well-founded, and not mere idle chatter, e.g., 'With a voice like yours you could be famous. Why don't you go to London, find a good teacher, and audition at Covent Garden?' A young singer's head is easily turned, and this sort of irresponsible advice is sure to cause trouble, particularly if he acts in the age-old way: gives up a job, comes to the metropolis with little money, wanders from one teacher to another, works hard for an audition and receives a few encouraging words as sole compensation. As for Mr. or Mrs. Counsellor, they will have forgotten the advice as soon as they uttered it, and probably their victim's name as well.

Advice needs to be concrete and responsible, e.g., 'I have a good friend in London who is in the music business. I'll write to him about you, and let you know what he says.' It is natural enough for young singers to ask advice of reputable performers, but it can sometimes produce unfortunate results. Singers who have had experience and success in one field are often unable to judge from their own viewpoint. Singer X, for instance, may have had natural assets, have met the right people and used his opportunities well. His advice will be quite different from singer Y's who has made his career the hard way. Some are too busy with their own careers to bother about the struggles of young singers, and are also often jealous. Others are so subjective that in spite of good intentions their advice is useless.

If advice is needed, it is better to collect several opinions and then make up one's mind on the basis of the majority recommendation: OR, ask no one at all. Reading several criticisms about an actor or singer may help form a balanced judgment, whereas a single criticism may be taken over as one's personal view.

Young students are often extremely biased in their advice to their colleagues. They may try to make them leave their present teachers saying that their own are better, whether or not this is true. They are seldom capable of objective judgment. The advice of an envious student seems to come from the heart, but is really meant to create confusion. It is like the jealous cat in the fairy tale, who flattered a centipede and then asked which foot he used first—first, second or third? Could he sometimes start on the 389th foot and follow with No. 17? From then on the centipede could walk no more.

Of course much advice is sound. Giovenale Sacchi (1726–1789), the music historian, provides an example in his biography of Carlo Broschi (Farinelli). After an extraordinary success in Italy, the famous castrato, in 1731 visited the Austrian Court. The Emperor, Karl VI, was a great music lover. He accompanied Farinelli on the clavichord, and then suggested that he work for expression as well as for dazzling effects. 'Your singing is unequalled' said the Emperor, 'but sing a simple melody now and again, and you will conquer the hearts of your audience as well as winning their admiration.' Fortunately Farinelli followed this good advice. He was to move even his colleague and rival,

Senesino, to tears, when the latter heard him for the first time.

I have been much helped by good advice in the course of my career. When I had acquired a certain reputation as a singer and teacher, I was fortunate enough to sing for Richard Strauss, who accompanied me himself. He made some favourable comments about my technique and expression, then said: 'You should watch the intervals in the higher middle range when you are singing legato. You are not exactly off pitch, but if you were a violinist or cellist I would tell you to tune your instrument more carefully. Have you noticed how a piano which has not been tuned for some time will sound better afterwards?' Your voice will have a much better sound if you learn to do this.' Although I had been singing with experienced conductors and coaches, not one had discovered this trouble, and I soon realised how right Strauss was. Many years later, I met him again by chance on a solitary Alpine walk, and was glad of the chance to thank him. I was also able to act on the advice given me by artists such as Battistini, Alessandro Bonci and Leo Slezak, which I could apply to my teaching as well as to my own singing.

Especially interesting and instructive were the remarks of Angelo Neumann, on the occasion of an audition when I was starting my career as an opera singer. Neumann became famous when already in 1878 he travelled with his own company performing Wagner's 'Ring des Nibelungen.' 'There is only one thing I don't like,' Neuman said on that occasion, 'Your voice sounds much older than you are. This is not a good sign. A healthy person always looks younger than his years, and a singer should sound younger too. In my opinion, the cause is your head resonance, and you should try to overcome this fault while you are still young.'

Performers who are given careful advice by the knowledgeable and trustworthy are truly fortunate.

'The pleasure of criticism deprives
us of the pleasure of being moved
by beautiful things.'

THE HABIT OF CRITICISM   JEAN DE LA BRUYERE (1688)
                                                         Caracteres II.

'It is much easier to be critical than
to be correct.'

DISRAELI: Speech in the House of
Commons. 24.1.1860

Many people enjoy criticising a performance more than enjoy-
ing it. They think this shows their musical understanding, but
it is a corroding habit, whereas a genuine reaction of pleasure is
stimulating. A group of friends meet after an inspiring operatic
performance, full of enthusiasm and eager to share their pleasure
with others. They are the ideal audience, and their delight is
threefold: they look forward to the experience, they enjoy it
when it happens, and they relish the memory of it. Along comes
Mr. Opposite wanting at all costs to disagree, and to take a stand
against the majority view. If majority opinion is positive about
a certain singer, he will mention details he disliked. Often he
does not pass a personal judgment but declares that X is not a
good singer, or that Y is not a good opera. He 'kills' one artist
with the memory of another, most likely already dead. As most
of the company knows nothing of this singer, Mr. Opposite has
no difficulty in belittling the performance they approve. Such
pseudo-connoisseurs always give the impression of being well-
informed.

Young singers may well be led astray by such people. They
should learn instead from a singer's good points, not through
picking holes in performances. This is not to say they should
not express an opinion, but that tact is a great virtue in a back-
biting profession. Very few singers can afford the luxury of

excessive criticism. One never knows who is listening, nor who is able to help or harm. The important thing is to enjoy the performances of other artists, and to learn from them.

I once had a contract for a year as 'eighth' baritone in a leading German opera house. I naturally spent most of my evenings in the 'Künstler Loge', a large box kept for members of the company. Baritones Nos. 1 and 2 had big reputations, and of course each claimed to be No. 1. At *Rheingold* one evening I was in the box with No. 2 when No. 1 was singing Wotan. He asked me what I thought of No. 1. As I was the youngest member of the company I judiciously remarked 'I think he is a first-class artist.' 'You are right', said no. 2. 'But have you noticed how he forces in the middle range, so that his high notes are not as big as they might be for his size of voice?' I politely agreed with him, particularly as it was a true comment. The next evening was *Die Walküre*. Nos. 1 and 2 sang Wotan alternatively, so that No. 1 was in the box whilst No. 2 was on stage. At the end of Act II, I was again asked my opinion. 'I think he is a great artist', I answered sincerely. 'Yes', said No. 1 'but let him be a warning to you. When I was your age, I made the same mistake as he is making now. I forced my middle range, so that my top notes did not sound big enough. I've got rid of that now!'

What is the moral of that little tale? As mentioned in 'How a singer hears himself' (p. 38), nobody can hear himself properly. What is more, it is foolish to criticise others for what we may be doing ourselves.

How far naive and impertinent criticism can go comes out in a story about Verdi. *Aida* was being enthusiastically received all over the world, when Verdi received a letter from a man in a small Italian town, who had gone to see it in Parma. He wrote that he did not like the opera. He had gone a second time but in spite of its good decor it still disappointed him. He informed Verdi that after a few more performances, *Aida* would disappear into the limbo of the libraries. As he was poor and father of a family, he considered that Verdi should reimburse him for the two expeditions and listed his expenses down to the last lira—trips, tickets, and two bad dinners at the station.

Tongue in cheek, Verdi told his publisher to reimburse the man for the journey and the theatre tickets, but not for the meals, in return for a written promise that he would never listen to another Verdi opera. Back came the answer, certifying that he would never go again unless he were paid *all* his expenses. Not even an outstanding composer can avoid being foolishly criticised by his audience! Ironically enough, it was Verdi who once remarked that for 3 lire the public buys the right to criticise. But where singing is concerned, it is much wiser for a young performer to keep a still tongue in his head.

SUCCESS MAY BE DANGEROUS,   'Success hath ruin'd many a man.'
FAILURE A BLESSING   BENJAMIN FRANKLIN:
                                             Poor Richard's Almanac, 1792.

As in all professions, some can reach their goal relatively easily, whilst others have many obstacles to overcome. Sometimes they forget to search deep enough for the reasons for their failure, which may depend on their own talents and actions as well as on other people and difficult circumstances.

Artists who have to struggle to reach success after failure are unquestionably in a stronger position than those who start their careers with great triumphs. The latter often decline and fail to live up to their reputations. The French soprano Cornelia Falcon is a case in point. Her premature success deceived operatic connoisseurs as well as herself. In 1832 she made her debut at the early age of 20 at the Grand Opera in Paris in the dramatic role of Alice in Meyerbeer's *Robert le Diable*. She was partnered by the famous dramatic tenor Nourrit and the heavy bass

Levasseur, who had taken part in the first performance. At twenty-three she created the dramatic soprano part of Rachel in Halévy's *La Juive*: at twenty-four she sang Valentine in the first performance of Meyerbeer's *Les Huguenots*. Her partners for both these operas were Nourrit and Levasseur. She was twenty-five when she sang the leading role in Niedermeyer's *Stradella* at the Grand Opera, and discovered, during the perform-ance, that she was losing her voice. The audience was informed, and the curtain came down forever on a magnificent career.

Cornelia Falcon spent the rest of her life—60 years—mourning her tragic failure, for in spite of many attempts she was unable to resume her career. Her tragic case is still quoted in France as a warning to young singers who want to appear in dramatic roles too soon. (cf. 'Lyric or Dramatic'.)

Another case is that of Marion Talley. At fifteen she gave a promising audition at the Metropolitan and made her debut three years later as Gilda in *Rigoletto*. Irving Kolodin relates the rest in his interesting book 'The Metropolitan Opera' (O.U.P., New York, 1933).

'Marion Talley's first appearance, in *Rigoletto*, was the signal for an outpouring of two hundred Kansas citizens, who trooped eastward en masse to support the native daughter. Although the Metropolitan cannot be held responsible for this demonstration— more becoming to a football team than to an opera singer—Otto Kahn had gone to the length of inviting Mayor Walker to share his box. Moreover, the management had permitted the Associ-ated Press to install a direct wire back stage, over which Talley senior—a telegrapher by trade—tapped out to the world his impression of his daughter's debut! It was the majority opinion of the professional listeners present that Talley possessed vocal material which, with culture, might have developed to reasonable usefulness; but the account, on the front page of the nation's newspapers, of the 4,200 persons within the auditorium and of the added hundreds without, (betrayed) the true character of the event, and of the singer. Talley was valuable to the Metropolitan as long as she was front page news; when she passed from that class, her career at the Metropolitan also declined. In the first performance with her were Lauri-Volpi, de Luca, Mardones, and Alcock. The conductor was Serafin.'

Previous to her debut, Talley was sent to Marcella Sembrich for preparatory work. After the teacher had heard the prospective pupil and formulated her opinion of the ground work that had to be done, she outlined a programme of vocal exercises, scales, technical studies, etc. Talley informed the great artist that all she wanted was 'coaching' in certain operatic roles, whereupon Sembrich declared that the interview was over, and dismissed her.

Truly great artists on the other hand have often had to work hard to overcome failure during their first years of singing. One has only to think of biographies of Caruso, Chaliapin and others. As Nietzsche said 'What does not knock me down makes me stronger'.

WHY DO PROFESSIONAL
SINGERS GO ON TAKING
LESSONS?

Learning is ever young, even in old age.

AESCHYLUS. *Agamemnon,* 790 B.C.

I am sorry that I have to leave the earth with 89 years, since I have just started to understand the fundamental facts of my art.

MICHELANGELO

People often wonder why professional singers, and successful ones at that, will go to a teacher for further study. As one who has often worked with such singers, I would like to emphasise that they need quite different treatment from the average student, even though they may have worse defects than some beginners. Far more is needed than a number of run-of-the-mill exercises which form the backbone of the average curriculum.

What prompts a singer to seek advice? The same reason that sends a sick man to a doctor, or a car owner to the garage mechanic. There is something wrong, and the cause may be anything at all. A singer's voice may change considerably with time. At thirty or forty, he can sing parts which were beyond him as a student. Sometimes the change is so great that he is not able to adjust himself to it without expert help. Instrumentalists are rarely faced with this sort of situation. A pianist, say, of fifty may have utterly changed since he was a young man, but his piano has not changed at all. Nor would he think of giving his first important recital until he had mastered most of the standard works for his instrument. But a singer—particularly one with a good voice—will often make a successful debut with a comparatively limited repertoire, and an unfinished technique. A pretty girl with a pleasant, half-trained voice can make a hit even before connoisseurs, but a young pianist could not hope to impress the same people without years of intensive study to his credit. As long as a voice is young and fresh, its defects are overlooked. As the singer gets older, the public gets more critical, and the defects are more pronounced. This makes him nervous and unsure of himself, and his performance gets worse. It is a vicious circle. No outsider can fully appreciate the mental torture a successful singer can suffer if mental or physical handicaps prevent him from singing certain passages as both he and his public expect.

It is hard enough for a beginner to find the right teacher, but it is even harder for the practising artist. He will say to himself 'Can he help me? Will his method be what I am used to? Won't he confuse more than help? Will he try and influence my style and general approach?' and, worst of all, 'won't he go round telling everybody I am a 'pupil' of his, so as to get himself publicity?' He may well look enviously at colleagues who can still go to the teacher who originally trained them, as a patient turns to his family doctor who knows his strong and weak points.

It is risky for a singer to change his technique radically when he is professionally active, especially if his voice has already suffered damage from improper use. Sometimes I have had to refuse to work with singers because they could not stop singing in public for the amount of time (generally a matter of months) needed to put their defects right. But when there is nothing serious to correct, a teacher can work while an artist continues his career. Still, caution is needed even in comparatively simple cases, for a singer may suffer moments of utter bewilderment in actual performance as to which technique to use—the old one which has proved inadequate but which has served for years, or the new one he is in process of mastering. Full confidence has to be established, for if the singer does not believe in the new method either, he will feel completely at sea. He may start going from one teacher to another from lack of trust. It is bad enough when a beginner does this, but it spells ruin for a practising singer. Teachers call such pupils 'wanderers'. Back in Vienna, a 'wanderer' like this came to me for help. He was a well-known heroic tenor at the State Opera House, but his voice had suffered irreparable damage from years of faulty technique and excessive tinkering by many teachers. When he sang a Wagnerian role, even the audience realised that he was switching from one way of singing to another, never sure of himself in any. Difficult as the decision was, I declined to work with him. As it turned out, it was a wise decision, because not many months later he retired aged less then fifty. I would have been the last to work on his voice, and would probably have been blamed for the premature end to his career. It was too late for any teacher to remedy the situation.

Sometimes a singer will come to a teacher because he wants to learn a new range of roles (the far-reaching change from baritone to tenor, or mezzo-soprano to soprano is discussed in chapter 7). I am thinking more of the change involved when a singer wants to switch over from lyric to dramatic parts, or from concert work to opera, or vice versa.

It goes without saying that a teacher must be scrupulously discreet about anyone who comes to him for further study, or to correct some defect. If the audience discovers it, they will tend to criticise defects they would never have noticed—which clearly does the singer no good. At one time three singers at the Vienna Opera were working with me. None of them knew that the others were studying with me. I managed to keep the secret so well that they never discovered it, although they were rehearsing and singing together as the three Rhine daughters in *Rheingold* and *Götterdämmerung*!

The best-known example of a successful singer who went to a teacher for further study is the Swedish Jenny Lind (see 'Middle Register', p. 86). Many years later, Leo Slezak also went to Paris to study with Jean de Reszke for six months. Slezak's pilgrimage, like Jenny Lind's, was amply repaid. When he came back to the Vienna Opera he was to become an internationally famous tenor. I mention this happy collaboration because it was Slezak who helped me when I was a young singer, and Jean de Reszke whose advice and patronage started me on my career as a teacher.

BETTER AN ARTISTIC	Singing is so good a thing I wish
AMATEUR THAN AN	all man would learn to sing.
AMATEURISH PROFESSIONAL	WILLIAM BYRD (1573–1623).

It is said that when as an unknown young man Disraeli was asked what he wanted to become, he answered simply 'Prime Minister of England'. In their young years many famous singers planned their careers, though nothing is heard of those who never made the grade. Some unsuccessful authors and composers console themselves with the excuse that many operas and plays later hailed as excellent works started life as failures. Students who want to become professional singers should be reminded that in these days voice and singing ability alone cannot ensure success: physical stamina and financial backing, determination to face hardships and setbacks, plus a good dose of luck are all too necessary. (Chapter 'How to become . . .' surveys the possibilities.)

There will always be singers who prefer to be artistic amateurs rather than amateurish professionals. Professionals who depend on a steady income seldom have savings or income from other sources. They often have to do violence to their artistic principles in order to make a living. They may have to appear with a half-prepared performance, or sing music which does not measure up to their standards. A person who prefers to earn his living in another profession often devotes himself to the cause of singing more effectively than many professionals. He sings whatever pleases him, enjoys himself more, and gives his self-selected audience unaffected pleasure.

HEALTH   The cautious seldom make mistakes.
                                    CONFUCIUS: Analects IV, *c.* 5 B.C.

Good vocal health obviously depends greatly on general health. 'Mens sana in corpore sano' might well read 'A healthy *voice* in a healthy body'. One senses if something is seriously wrong with the voice. It is like driving a familiar car—a dangerous rattle or squeak is recognised straight away.

All too often, non-singers remark disparagingly that 'singers are hypochondriacs anyway—forever coddling themselves'. Shrug off any such slurs! For most people a slight cold or sore throat means a disagreeable inconvenience; for the singer it is something far more vital. A slight indisposition may harm an entire career. Far too often, careers have been thwarted because a singer could not give his best or was unable to sing on an evening when influential people were present. A singer needs to be known as a reliable singer as well as a good one, and often obtains work for this reason. A management does not offer long-term contracts to singers who frequently cancel their performances because of poor health.

Eating, Drinking and Smoking

Avoid singing too soon after a meal, though at the other extreme, many singers feel weak if they work on an empty stomach.

Avoid ice-cold drinks, especially just after singing. Sipping ice-cream sodas through a straw strikes directly against the palate, whereas ice cream warms to body temperature as it melts in the mouth. This is good advice, though singer X will declare that he drinks what he likes, whenever he likes, with no ill effects. Reams of advice have been written about alcoholic excess. Singers often say they sing better if they drink something before coming on stage. But alcohol is apt to dry the mucous membranes, which instead need lubricating. The natural nervousness before performing tends to dry the throat, and this is accentuated by the heat of the stage lights. Beer is a possible exception because of the malt in it. Other things beside alcohol make a throat feel relaxed, and keep the mucous membranes moist. A singer should gargle with bicarbonate of soda in a little lukewarm water, or drink a little hot milk. Both are good, mild remedies. Some singers use dry prunes, soft apples, and hot tea. The individual singer will have to experiment. He should be careful about cough drops and throat lozenges, which may help one and harm another. Many are medicated with menthol, which is fine for people with too much mucous: if a singer has an over-dry throat, however, it is useless to take something which dries it still more. If alcohol is used as an emotional stimulant, the advice against it still stands. It is not the alcohol which is dangerous; it is the reliance upon the alcohol. Like drug addiction, alcohol seems to demand ever-increasing doses to retain its effectiveness as a stimulant.

Smoking: Caruso was a heavy smoker. When I am told this, I reply: 'Caruso had so many good qualities. Why not try imitating *them* instead?' It does not prove that heavy smoking is required for good singing. A few doctors still declare the habit not harmful, but they are generally smokers themselves, as witness the following story: A doctor told a convalescent patient that he could allow him one cigar after dinner. Two days later, he asked him how he felt. 'Fine', the man said, 'but I don't feel so good after that one cigar business. I've always been a non-smoker.'

Singers often claim that smoking 'improves their resonance' or 'disinfects their throat and nose'; but their wish is father to their excuse, though it is clearly worse for some than for others. Only ardent smokers and tobacco distributors claim that smoking is innocuous. The mucous membranes of trachea, bronchi, larynx and pharynx are endangered by heavy smoking, as is the whole body.

Limited Exercise

No exercise or sport should be carried to the point of fatigue. An hour's walking is a good idea in good weather, preferably in gardens, parks or quiet streets. Even this may be dangerous for a singer, if he tries to talk against a high wind. Walking in gentle rain may be highly beneficial, as long as the shoes are strong and the clothing adequate. Even better is a walk *after* it has rained, when the air has been purified.

Indoor Exercise: Be careful not to go out too soon after a game of squash, or table tennis. It is very easy to catch cold after perspiring heavily.

Temperature Changes, Climate: Italians say 'Il sole di marzo fa male' (The March sun is dangerous): it is deceptive, and not as hot as it seems. Equally, a singer walking in the warm sunshine may suffer too sharp a change when he returns to the cold rooms of his house. Such hazards are increased by air conditioning, which keeps interior temperatures degrees higher or lower than the outside air. It provides excellent opportunities for catching colds. Another fine way is to come out of a hot theatre with an uncovered head after wearing a wig.

Clearing the Throat:[1] This seemingly innocent procedure may be harmful if it is done in the usual forced way. A singer should clear his throat by using his diaphragm, gently expelling the phlegm by air pressure, rather than by straining the cords and throat muscles. (See Forcing, etc.)

Coughing is also dangerous, as it strains the vocal cords, often in a perilous way. It is the second or third stage of a bad throat condition, i.e., a neglected cold turns into a cough. A singer should do his best to cure a cold before it gets severe. Every coughing fit jeopardizes the elasticity of the vocal cords. Nobody can look after his voice as a violinist takes care of his violin—in a box covered with a silk handkerchief whenever it is not in use —but he can take care to own a healthy instrument.

Avoiding and Getting Rid of Colds

The bedroom is very important. Sleeping with open windows is not to be recommended unless one is accustomed to the climate. The bed should not be too close to an open window in case of sharp temperature changes during the night. The room should be well ventilated during the day unless the air is heavy with fog or damp. In air-conditioned houses, if the bedroom air is

---

[1] I once watched Alessandro Bonci preparing for a concert. He patiently sang exercises for more than an hour, though phlegm was obviously disturbing him. When he finished, I suggested that clearing his throat would help him. Bonci laughed and said, 'Do you take me for a coachman? He can clear his throat as much as he wants. Clearing the throat for a singer is as hard as slamming your wrist-watch down on a table.'

too dry when going to bed, it is a good plan to hang a damp sheet near the bed; the sheet will have dried out by morning, but the sleeper's throat will not. In hot, dry climates, keep bedroom air moist, particularly if a cold is threatening. If the nostrils get uncomfortably dry, a little vaseline inserted in each nostril before going to bed is slowly absorbed during the night, and the passages feel pleasantly clear and moist by morning.

If after every reasonable precaution, a singer catches cold, he should act promptly. The slightest sympton should be treated at once so as to speed recovery. He should, if possible, remain in the same temperature and if he has a fever he should go to bed. This simple treatment often does more good than widely advertised remedies. If the cold persists, it is a wise precaution to consult a throat specialist. A head cold is less harmful than a cold in the throat, because the nostrils provide natural means of draining away the excess fluid. With proper precautions there is small danger of it spreading to the throat, and it usually clears up in a day or two. It is unwise to use strong nasal inhalants. There will be a sense of relief through prompt drying up and clearing of the passages, but the infection may pass into more serious areas—the sinuses or throat.

In the past, some opera singers used to take a pinch of snuff before their performances, inducing a sneeze which cleared the nostrils. Perhaps there is sound reasoning behind saying 'Gesundheit' if somebody sneezes in your presence; it is a natural way of getting rid of an irritant.

Singers sometimes disagree about the effects of colds. Herman Klein, in *Thirty Years of Musical Life in London* relates how Tamagno once had a slight cold in his chest, but insisted that it made no difference to the quality of his head notes. 'Catarrh in the nose' he said, 'is fatal, but a chest cold makes not the slightest difference to me'. A good singer with a sound technique can sing on a cold. After one of Gigli's recitals in Vienna, I went to congratulate him as usual. The man guarding the green-room door said that Gigli had influenza and a high temperature and did not want to infect his visitors. I was flabbergasted, as I had not noticed the slightest change in his singing, proof of how well his physical equipment was under control. A doctor would naturally never advise a singer to perform in this condition: yet with knowledge of his patient he might make an exception.

Tonsils and Tonsillitis

Frequent colds, accompanied by a sore throat, tonsillitis and enlarged neck glands are signs that an operation is essential, and avoiding it can cause trouble. Will the operation harm the voice? Tonsillectomy definitely does *not* affect the voice or technique. In forty years of teaching I have never heard of any ill effects.

Before Performances: It is best to talk as little as possible before strenuous performances and rehearsals, and be as silent as possible on days when one has to sing a difficult role or a long concert. Avoid needless excitement, and stay out of loud arguments. Even a protracted telephone conversation is bad. Crying or loud laughing is also bad for the voice, although life may force both these emotional strains upon a singer.

After the Performance: What a singer does when the performance is over is as important as how he looks after himself before. He should stay in the same temperature for a reasonable time, then go home to bed. A lukewarm bath is good after a strenuous opera role.

After a taxing performance, I would soak a towel in lukewarm water, wrap it round my neck and cover it with a heavy dry towel. Before getting up in the morning, I would remove the wet towel, and wrap the dry towel round my throat for a while. One should not get addicted to this, but it is an excellent remedy which was suggested to me in my youth by a famous singer, and I pass it on for what it is worth.

But to be too careful of every draught is as foolish as being careless. Keep to the golden mean!

Emotional Upsets

A singer is a human being, with 'organs, dimensions, senses, affections and passions' like everyone else. He often has greater sensitivity than the average person, and lives on a plane of heightened emotional intensity. No wonder if his voice reflects his state of mind; if he is seriously upset by deep grief or anger, it is often impossible to suggest a remedy. It is better not to sing when one is in this sort of state. A singer with a sound technique may manage to perform in spite of a bad physical condition, but it is tempting providence to sing when he is really over-wrought. The wise singer will avoid performing if he is under intense emotional strain.

Vocal Long Life: The life of a voice depends on how it has been treated. Sometimes a ten-year-old car is in better condition than a two-year-old model. Patti sang for forty-seven years in public, and as Herman Klein remarks in his book:[1]

'To analyse the secret of Patti's voice one can only say; here surely is a singer of marvellous constitution, heaven-gifted with a faultless method, who has sedulously nursed her physical resources and has never under any circumstances imposed the smallest undue strain upon the exquisitely proportioned mechanism of her vocal organs.'

Sex and the Voice

> *Even nectar is poison if taken to excess*: Hindu Proverb.

In the course of a long teaching career, I have always encouraged students to feel free to ask questions about anything

[1] *Thirty Years of Musical Life in London*, p. 4.

connected with their work as singers. On several occasions young girls have asked whether in my opinion sexual intercourse is necessary or beneficial in the development of the voice. This particular question has always been the subject of much animated discussion in private, but it is rarely touched on in books on singing.

In this case as in so many controversial matters, the answer to this question cannot be a simple 'yes' or 'no'. Among my students, there have been young women whose would-be lovers have assured them that sex will do wonders for the voice. Should she, the young girl asks, 'make the sacrifice' for the sake of her voice? Such a rationalisation is naive and largely irrelevant. That the question is asked in the first place probably indicates that the girl is neither ready nor willing to embark on a sexual relationship.

Physical changes and emotional upheavals affect the voice in much the same way as they do other parts of the body, and to a greater or lesser degree in different people. There are no specific rules. All phases of a woman's sexual life—the onset of menstruation, the loss of virginity, pregnancy, childbearing, the menopause—may have some noticeable effect on the voice as on the physical appearance and emotional balance of the individual.

Sometimes one may come across a young girl with a voice of such richness and maturity, that to hear her sing without seeing her childlike face and body, one would think her voice belonged to a woman of at least thirty. A coloratura soprano on the other hand may retain the immature quality of a young girl's voice, even after years of marriage and childbearing.

As a singing teacher I have noticed only one common characteristic in the voices of girls who have had no sexual experience. The tones between the F in the chest register and the C or D in the middle register are often weak. These weaker tones usually develop as the girl matures. Incidentally, in most cases it is these same tones that weaken first in singers who have passed the period of menopause. When such singers use their voices *mezza voce* or *piano* they are often able to overcome this weakness, but when they sing these tones in a full, dramatic way, the voice wavers and falters, and the best technique is unable to overcome this defect. Even the singing art of the great Lilly Lehmann was incapable of surmounting this obstacle when she sang in her later years.

The teacher, working with a student for several years, naturally becomes familiar with every slight nuance of her voice. If the girl feels happy or sad, or is perhaps ill, this will all be reflected in her voice. If the middle tones are weak, great care must be taken to avoid strenuous exercises which could damage the voice irreparably.

Apart from the gradual maturing of the middle tones, it is probably the psychological impact of a sexual relationship that has the most noticeable effect on the voice. When a young woman becomes involved in an unhappy love affair, her singing will suffer. A happy and successful relationship on the other hand can have as positive and beneficial effect on the voice as on the whole personality. If a singer is living a full and happy life without sexual relations, there is no reason to believe that sex would automatically bring about a miraculous improvement in the voice. Neither sex nor anything else can be a substitute for the hard work necessary in acquiring a good singing technique— the only true way of improving the voice.

As far as men are concerned, in relation to sex, I can only refer them to the Hindu proverb heading this chapter.

COACHES AND CONDUCTORS

'The real task of a conductor is to make himself clearly unnecessary; we are pilots and not rowers.'

FRANZ LISZT

The vocal coach is indispensable for teachers who cannot play the piano. Some teachers cannot even accompany elementary exercises, and need an accompanist from the very beginning. But those who are good at accompanying are greatly helped by a coach who can work with advanced students on musical preparation. Premature handing-over to a coach may be dangerous, as the coach is only concerned with musical accuracy and not with the voice itself. A good coach must be a good pianist, able to play everything, if possible, at sight. He must be able to handle singers and also give them a lead. The more he knows about singing the better.

An operatic conductor has to teach his singers in rehearsal, and in performance achieve complete coordination between singers and orchestra. Both coaches and conductors have an important role to play in developing singers, but sometimes they are more hindrance than help. Working with singers requires an inborn talent, and a desire to understand their problems. Conductors need to be sensitive to a singer's physical limits (of range, breath, etc.). They must know if a singer needs easing over a difficult passage, and realise that he is dependent on his physical condition, which may vary even during the performance itself. He may tell a singer he does not want to work with him again; but he must never let him down on the night. In cases of dispute, it is often difficult to know who is right, but both singer and conductor have to cooperate. An unmusical singer will always find it difficult to understand a conductor's viewpoint. Equally, a coach or conductor who has no feeling for singing will seldom be aware of a singer's potentialities.

How do future coaches and conductors prepare for their exacting professions? In a good music school, where they study piano, harmony and counterpoint, etc., and enjoy the leadership of an experienced conductor with a flair for teaching. During this formative period it is always good to work in close collaboration with a singing teacher so as to learn as much as possible about the voice. Countless conductors have started in opera houses as coaches (repetiteurs) who accompany stage rehearsals; from there they are lucky if they can gravitate to assisting an outstanding conductor—as Bruno Walter worked for Gustav Mahler.

Some try and persuade singers to undertake unsuitable parts, and easily jump to wrong conclusions. They will say to a young singer: 'X sang this part with me in his early days before he became famous and (false conclusion) you have the same sort of voice as he had when he began.' There may well be some resemblance, but though a voice sounds similar it will never be exactly the same. The difference may be one of physique or technique; it may even have been bad for the first singer to have sung the role as a beginner, so that he narrowly missed being harmed by it, i.e., he succeeded in spite of it.

This is not a general criticism, but is intended to show that coaches and conductors need to have a very clear idea of their responsibilities, and a basic knowledge of singing.

THE MICROPHONE A
BLESSING AND A DANGER

> An exact and individual record of the voices of our great prime donne (should such a thing become possible) would not only profit their own celebrity, but would open the road directly to vast and unlooked-for progress in the art of singing as a whole.
>
> STENDHAL: Life of Rossini (publ. 1824). *Sic*.

The microphone is certainly a blessing for singers, but it can be a menace if it is allowed to compensate for lack of technique. To take an extreme example, a night-club singer who hugs a mike so tenderly would be quite lost without his loudspeaker.

Constant microphone-singing does the voice no good, and it is best to use it indirectly if at all, i.e., when microphones are installed on the stage of large halls or in an open-air stadium, etc.

Many people are not fully aware what a microphone can do for the voice. They regard it as a magical talisman which can transform a poor voice into a beautiful one, whereas it is only able to amplify a small sound (*mikros,* small, *phonos,* sound). It is a miracle-worker for small voices with a clearly-defined timbre, who could not reach large audiences without it. Some sound better in broadcasts than in nature (e.g. well-built basses and baritones, and many tenors), others (e.g. high sopranos) sound less well. The sound is often quite different in large broadcast performances; this depends on where the singer is standing in relation to the microphone, as the balance of voices in an ensemble may be totally different from the way they are heard in an opera-house; and whether there has been time for the singers to 'mix' their tone with that of the other performers. (In record making, several takes are made.) In general, the bigger the voice, the greater the skill needed in projecting it. But there should be no basic change in production. A microphone is a magnifying mirror for defects or temporary voice complaints. A cold can sometimes be disguised when singing with an orchestra, but not with a microphone.

It is good for a student to hear himself frequently on a tape machine, especially when his teacher is present. He can hear himself as others hear him and learn to judge his voice more objectively. This idea was well-known long before the invention of the microphone. At the end of the 16th century the Roman teacher Fedi led his pupils to a well-known spot near San Paolo with an echo, where they sang and listened to themselves. A singer can use records for memorising, or play a single phrase over and over again, learning much in style, phrasing, expression and so on. But not every record is authentic, and well-known singers use plenty of tricks to hide their weaknesses, which to imitate would be fatal. Many young singers try out their voices by singing with records, a highly dangerous proceeding. But for general listening purposes the benefit of classical recordings is incalculable. Even in great centres like Vienna it was impossible to hear the great symphonies and operas more than once or twice a year. Thanks to hi-fi, one can hear in comfort at home, performances which are not all that different from those heard in discomfort in the gods.

Old records are a continual delight in spite of their imperfections. Edison perfected the wax cylinder in 1888, and the first flat disc was experimentally used in 1896 and put to commercial use in 1900. Caruso made his first records in the United States on November 23, 1903, shortly after his debut at the Metropolitan. He recorded ten arias, all in one afternoon and all only once. (These included *Celeste Aida*, two arias from *Rigoletto*, Manrico's *stretto* from *Trovatore* and his famous *Tosca* aria, etc.) Only at later recording sessions did he sing one aria several times. Caruso's baritone-like tenor with ringing top notes was an ideal voice for records. Women's voices, orchestras, piano and other instruments were impossible to record. Some singers (e.g., Theodore Reichmann) refused to allow his records to go on sale because he was unsatisfied with the sound of his voice. Francesco Tamagno on the other hand was reputedly enthusiastic about his records, and the tenor Leo Slezak also made successful early records. Patti made hers when she was over sixty, and the results were disappointing. People who actually heard famous singers in the flesh are willing to overlook the noises and poor recording technique of their records, but those who did not cannot supply from their memory what is missing. Comparison with modern recording and records is a futile pursuit. But connoisseurs will still enjoy listening to Chaliapin's records (particularly *Boris Godunov* and *Song of the Volga Boatmen*), to Caruso, to Battistini:

and many others. It is sad that the great Lieder singer Johannes Meschaert (q.v.) never recorded his authentic interpretations of songs by Schubert, Schumann, Brahms, etc.

Singing on Television

When a singer performs on TV, it is not so much for regular opera fans as for the millions who have never seen opera. Let him not scare them away with a facial expression at odds with the words he is singing. He *must* be free of tension, for he is seen as through a magnifying glass. If he tenses his mouth, his eyes will show it, as they always reflect forcing of any kind. As a special example of easy and natural-artistic singing I want to mention Theresa Berganza. Her tone emission is effortless, her eyes are able to express her feelings without being influenced by the work of her facial muscles. What was the secret of Buster Keaton's comedy? To keep the same sad eyes and face whatever the situation. A singer cannot often afford this sort of effect!

Can greater singers be expected as a result of so many technical aids? It does not seem so, for talent does not depend on technical processes. But the primary question remains: how can mechanical aids best be used to supplement the teacher's work?

'POP' SINGING

'Pop' singing does not really concern a book of this kind, but it does occasionally cross the path of 'serious' singing. 'Pop' singers have become an important element in social life. Their earning capacity and skyrocketing rise to success dazzles millions. They have helped to build the record business to what it is today.[1]

They are not a modern species: Ancient Greece most certainly had its popular entertainers. But Aeschylus, Sophocles and Euripides found an audience willing to listen to the tetralogies

---

[1] The author is aware that in criticising 'pop' singers he is trying to empty the sea with a spoon.

performed each year in honour of Dionysus for three days on end. The masses of those days may not have been so highly educated, but popular entertainment was certainly less obtrusive and less specialised than it is today. In Shakespeare's time noblemen and labourers alike packed the Globe Theatre to be entertained without needing text *or* commentary.

'Pop' singing received an unexpected fillip from the microphone. Previously popular entertainers could only appear before limited audiences because their voices could not be heard in large halls. Many could not be heard even in nightclubs without a microphone. (See Microphone chapter, p. 200.) Classical music too has gained enormously from recording, radio and television. Yet world-famous artists like Paganini, Liszt, Jenny Lind, Johann Strauss, de Reszke—to mention only a few—made their reputations without their help.

Nowadays music haunts us everywhere. Nearly every car has a radio installed, so that the driver can listen for hours. TV sets and juke boxes invade pubs and coffee-bars, larger restaurants have a band or a blaring radio. When 'modern man' arrives home, the radio is turned on if the telly is not on already. Some people go to bed with the radio on, others use it to wake themselves up. Many hesitate to leave the house without a portable radio—there may be a moment's quiet along the way. People are selective about what they eat but not about what they hear: they just long for uninterrupted sound-waves which they soak up as a car absorbs petrol. It has become a habit, even an international calamity, that large groups of people cannot be without the sound of a popular tune. Popular music is manufactured on a vast scale for the un- or semi-musical, who are naturally in the majority, and include many highly intelligent people. So it is not difficult to understand why the industry is successful.

WHAT HAS ALL THIS TO DO WITH THE ART OF SINGING? Some students may well have moments of doubt.

Why work so hard for so long to develop a voice? Why try and learn such difficult music? Why struggle to make a living as a professional singer with the prospect of earning only a fraction of what a 'pop' singer can earn?

How can a teacher reply? He should never evade the issue, but rather add some questions of his own. Why does the head-waiter of a fashionable night-club earn disproportionately more than a barrister? Why does a race-horse owner often make more money in a day than Dr. Salk—whose vaccine can save millions of adults and children—can earn in years? Everyone is free to choose his own profession. If a student wants to become a 'pop' singer, it is certainly not a dishonourable profession. It is just an entirely different field.

With justice, opera singers have frequently been mocked for stereotyped gestures and awkward movements. But they generally compensate for their clumsiness by the quality of their singing. 'Pop' singers also have their stereotyped gestures. They start each musical phrase with the same characteristic nod and regular swinging of their arms. Women singers especially indicate the last note of a song by lifting their hands above their head. It is also in vogue to sing a well-known tune slightly out of tempo, or under the note. These clumsy efforts to hide failings are called STYLE. When a 'pop' singer is really amateurish in the way he overcomes them, HE CALLS HIMSELF A VOCAL STYLIST.

It should be added that many male crooners, such as Perry Como, Eddie Fisher or Bing Crosby, have an agreeable voice and use it in a simple way. Like the *castrati* of old, they only sing what suits their voices, and they do not try to sing higher notes than they can easily reach. Their way of singing would not endanger a young voice. But the horrible habit female 'pop' singers have

of forcing the chest register up to and higher is a

real menace for young girl students as well as an offence against good taste (see p. 62, 'Chest Register').

For commercial reasons in the United States, and to a growing extent in England, opera and concert singers often make junkets into the field of popular music. Artists like Lauritz Melchior, Jan Peerce and others often appear in night-clubs in Las Vegas, without endangering their voice or prestige. But they select songs which suit them, and generally bring the house down by their own hits, such as Canio's lament from *I Pagliacci,* etc. Helen Traubel gave up her relatively short operatic career to devote herself exclusively to 'pop' singing. She was already a mature singer when she made her debut at the Metropolitan, and her well-developed middle range, and skilful choice of high quality songs by Jerome Kern, etc., protect her from any ill effects. The younger and less experienced the singer, the more dangerous is an excursion into this field. Students who want to use their instrument for singing should avoid 'pop' music as far as possible, though it is possible to gain stage experience in musicals without coming to any harm, as they encourage a straightforward emission of the voice.

BASIC REQUIREMENTS

The younger generation often learns much too late that only a very small percentage of those who devote time and talent year after year to singing will be lucky enough to become professional singers, let alone make a living from it.

1.—*An Opera Singer*

People still think a good voice is all that is necessary for an opera singer. But he has to have at least five different qualities:

(*a*) a good, strong voice, and a healthy body,

(b) musical ability,

(c) intelligence and working capacity to develop voice and technique,

(d) good presentation (naturally there are exceptions),

(e) a certain talent for acting—

and a good teacher who follows his progress!

Very few singers earn a steady living in this field. They are classified as 'old' at fifty or fifty-five, an age which in other professions heralds a new period of achievement. It is tragic that singers have to stop when success, popularity and experience is at its zenith. A genuine opera singer is devoted to his profession body and soul, but he has to renounce success and a good income without feeling discarded. It is understandable that many cling to it and try to stay as long as they can. Many say they will stop singing before the audience hears the decline in their voice, but in practice this is not so easy. Edward Hanslik heard a pitiful decline in Jenny Lind's voice, which she overcame by sheer force of charm and skill. She confided to him that her voice was declining, but added 'with my technique I can always overcome my failings'. Hanslik was embarrassed and dared not contradict.

An opera singer never ceases to learn, and needs postgraduate study as much as a doctor or teacher. But how can he get it? Only by being with a regular operatic ensemble in which he is given parts which suit him. A conductor who works for years in the same opera house is anxious to develop the singer through progressively harder roles. He has an excellent chance of singing them several times within a few weeks or months, and in this way he can grow. He should also be prepared to give concerts and appear on radio and television, often with the same repertoire.

When Gustav Mahler became general manager and first conductor of the Vienna Imperial Opera, he was able to offer Leo Slezak a ten-year contract. The benefit was immense. In his early twenties, Slezak's gigantic appearance and large voice won him the role of Siegfried at the Royal Berlin Opera. Now he was given typically lyrical parts (Tamino in *Magic Flute*, Belmonte in *Seraglio* and even opera comique roles like George Brown in Auber's *Dame Blanche*) in addition to heavy roles such as Manrico in *Trovatore*, Arnold in *William Tell* and Walther in *Meistersinger*. He could maintain and develop his marvellous piano and mezza voce in the best traditions of *bel canto*, yet possess enough power for his dramatic top notes.

Nowadays this would be impossible. No outstanding singer would accept a ten-year contract, nor sing in only one opera house, even if it was a leading one. The amazing improvement in plane travel permits him to accept engagements all over the world, and he can visit different continents several times a year. Surprisingly enough, this is not an advantage. Opera singers need steady control, and rarely is their development helped by rushing from job to job and rehearsal to rehearsal under the baton of different conductors. Guest appearances are no way of helping either singer or conductor to work out a role, although they are a splendid and interesting source of income. Inevitably they shorten a singer's 'life', and a strange audience is merciless about the failings of an overworked singer; they merely want the best for their money. Opera in many countries is a matter of sensation, and singers have to live up to it.

Possibilities for opera singers are certainly more interesting and varied than before, but they are also much more destructive (see chapter: Are singers of today better than singers of the past?).

2.—A Concert Singer

Concert singers are of three types:

1. Opera singers who cannot sing opera the whole year round, and travel about giving concerts which include many of their successful arias.

2. Recitalists who choose the bulk of their repertoire from the standard songs of a particular country (e.g. French, German, Russian, etc.) and songs by contemporary composers. They may also include much out-of-the-way music from lesser-known periods, and folk-music, ballads, etc. Those with true lyric quality in their voices are outstandingly successful in this field, though their programmes seldom have the artistic unity of the dedicated Lieder singer as their recitals need to be as varied as possible.

3. Recitalists who specialise in certain periods (modern, Elizabethan, etc.). Lieder singers devote their entire programme to German Lieder (Liederabende). Many successful opera singers often become fine Lieder singers (e.g. Leo Slezak, Lilly Lehmann), but it is rare for a fine Lieder singer to turn to opera.

General Needs. (*a*) A concert singer needs no more than an accompanist (but what an accompanist!), a piano and a hall large or small, accommodating 20 or 2,000: a well-trained voice, and a personality capable of interesting his audience. Once the demand is established, the opportunities, particularly in America, are great, and lead to radio and television appearances. In Europe the scope is more limited.

If a singer is doubtful about his choice of programme, he should consult the manager of the concert series. A famous singer will always choose his most successful songs even if the language is not that spoken by his audience.

A Word to the wise. (*b*) Do not give the impression of singing for effect. If a singer has good top notes, he should not appear to have chosen the song so as to show them off. If an encore is requested, it should be chosen in relation to what has gone before, i.e., not a negro spiritual after a Schumann Lied! Every appearance, however seemingly unimportant, may mean a 'break': a singer

*14

can never be sure who is in the audience. It is foolish to think 'There are only a few people in the audience, so I can take it easy.' This fatal attitude can easily become a habit. Whatever the type or size of audience, a singer should give his best.

Qualifications of the Genuine Recitalist and Lieder Singer

1. *A voice able to express the subtlest gradations of tone,* and a vocal technique even more perfect than an opera singer's: this is not often realised. He is far more exposed and his high notes must be sung without any facial distortion, for he is generally much closer to his audience. His face and eyes must accurately express the mood of his song.

2. *Language, diction and expression.* In the course of one evening, he has to change mood and expression twenty or more times, and do it so convincingly that he carries his audience along with him, whatever the language in which he is singing. He has to create his illusion without the help of any 'props' whatever.

3. *High cultural and musical background*—plus intelligence of no mean order. Complete understanding of the poetry of a song is essential. Just as a composer has to grasp the inner meaning of a poem before setting it, so a Lieder singer has to penetrate it imaginatively before he can 'recreate' it.

Advantages Over the Opera Singer

1. The voice is not so strained at the climaxes of the songs.
2. A singer can choose his own programme and avoid songs that do not suit him.
3. He can sing the songs in whatever order he wishes to present them. (Good programme-building is a great art.)
4. He can choose the key that suits him best.

Are Some Songs Meant only for Men?

It is beyond my comprehension why audiences will accept a

woman Lieder singer who pours out her heart in Strauss' *Traum durch die Dämmerung* ('Now I go to the most beautiful woman') and other such songs, clearly intended for men. Fischer Dieskau would cut a sorry figure if he sang *Gretchen am Spinnrade* or *Frauenliebe und Leben*, however perfectly he did it.

Chaliapin had a novel method of programme-building, which to my knowledge has not been imitated by any other well-known singer. He did not give his listeners a list of what he was going to sing, but distributed a booklet listing 125 songs with the complete text of the language in which he sang them. He would appear on stage, acknowledge the applause and carry on an animated conversation in whispers with his accompanist. He would then pick some songs from a huge pile of music on the piano. Sometimes he would change his mind and take another. Then would follow a silent dress rehearsal with his harassed pianist. He finally announced the number of the song, waited for the audience to page through the booklet to find it, and began to sing. This procedure was repeated after every song. When he thought it was time for an interval, he walked off stage. Unorthodox as it was, it suited a singer as sensitive as Chaliapin, and even those who resented it were soon won over and went along with him wholeheartedly.

The Perfect Accompanist

Verdi once said that mentally speaking an opera composer and his librettist should resemble a happily married couple. The same is true of a Lieder singer and his permanent accompanist. The good accompanist is a paragon of virtue, and does everything right without being in any way conspicuous. He needs a perfect piano technique—(in a way he is even more of a virtuoso than a solo pianist)—and he must be equal to every task of transposition, last moment adaptation and emergency cunning if the singer makes a mistake or jumps a few bars. Presence of mind is indispensable. He needs a thorough knowledge of singing and must understand his singer completely, have an instinctive feeling for his breath and help him if it is running short. He must give him time to prepare for a high note or phrase in a high tessitura without doing violence to the music. He must adapt himself to the singer's personality without sacrificing his own musical integrity. He must know when to follow and when to lead, when to submit and when to educate. He must scrupulously avoid drawing attention to himself by unusual facial expressions or flamboyant playing: he must neither drown the singer in a welter of sound nor play so quietly that he lacks support. To do this he needs to be a good judge of the acoustics of the hall. Over-effacing accompanists tend frequently to play too quietly with the left hand, and rob songs of their substance.

He must help a singer in rehearsal and performance, encourage and inspire him if he is dispirited. He can never permit himself any nerves, for it might affect the singer. A famous singer once said to me 'I'm shaky enough on stage as it is. I don't like to see the guy at the piano shake too.'

It is easy to see why fine accompanists are worth their weight in gold, and eagerly sought after by singers and managers. Few opera conductors manage to keep the necessary lightness of touch because of the vigorous control needed at opera rehearsals, but Bruno Walter has always been as great an accompanist as a conductor, and Richard Strauss was for years an excellent accompanist of his own songs, first for his wife, Pauline and later for Elizabeth Schumann and Franz Steiner.

3.—*A Church or Oratorio Singer*

The first requirement is good musicianship and a well-trained voice. He needs a good sense of style, never too theatrical, and he must avoid all 'operatic' effects. An oratorio singer has to sound 'serious', and his emotional intensity should always suit the solemnity of the music and the atmosphere of the building. The cantor in a Jewish synagogue is an exception to this rule. His singing demands more warmth and vocal brilliance. He is alone amongst 'liturgical' singers in that he receives a well-paid contract for several years, particularly when the congregation like him. Other creeds pay their singers, but not enough to make a living.

4.—A Musical Comedy Singer (Operettas, Musicals)

The first requisite is to be a good enough actor, and to be able to hold one's own in a straight play. Musical comedy does not ask too much of the voice, but the voice needs to be pleasant and easily produced. Speaking and singing need to be equalised as much as possible, so that one voice-placement will serve for many years. An actor who sings can continue to play older parts and need not retire like an opera singer. Although many successful players never studied speaking or singing, it is always advisable to have singing lessons from someone experienced in the musical comedy field.

5.—An Operatic Chorister

An unsuccessful soloist may decide to become a chorister. The more musical and linguistically versatile he is, the greater his chances. Musicals, light operas and operettas also need good choristers, and the work is often better paid than in opera. Chorus singers in operettas need to be musically reliable and able to sing well night after night. They sometimes get paid jobs in churches and oratorio choruses, especially if they are able to take over solo parts.

6.—A Commercial Singer

There are plenty of opportunities in radio, cinema, television and recording. Good quartet singers are particularly valuable, not only for performances in clubs and night-clubs, but also for advertising 'jingles'. Musicality, vocal ability and general reliability are important assets here too.

Many who study for pleasure can use their voices to add to their incomes. The wife of a well-to-do businessman once worked with me for some time, and her husband mockingly allowed her to give concerts now and then. When the family was forced to escape to Shanghai from Vienna she was able to supplement her husband's diminished earning-power by teaching, singing and performing in clubs.

Make Music With Your Voice

> 'To play an instrument correctly
> means to sing with it.'
>
> RICHARD WAGNER

The human voice is the only musical instrument which is not exclusively concerned in making music. On the contrary, most people are unaware they possess one. Generally, of course, they are not instruments which can make music, or at least not good music. Most voice-owners are unmusical and neither would nor could use them for music. What a blessing—even a melomane would go off his head if everyone decided to start music-making with his voice. But singers often forget that this is the point of singing. They intoxicate themselves with songs and arias, etc., hammering out loud notes or phrases. They think in terms of the single note, not of the phrase or the piece. A singer's real task is to transform the notes he makes, as a great author transforms the common words of his language. How he does it is what matters. As the Marschallin remarks in *Rosenkavalier* 'In dem Wie da liegt der ganze Unterschied'. (In the *How* lies the whole difference.)

CHAPTER 11

THE MICROPHONE
and
HEAD RESONANCE

Many voice students and singers, even some voice teachers, are unaware that the most effective amplifier is in the singer's own voice, his personal microphone—the head resonance. Admittedly, the head resonance can never amplify the human voice in a similar degree to the microphone sound system, but it has the tremendous advantage of beautifying, protecting and preserving the voice. The ancient Greeks in their classical plays knew that the voices of the actors had to be amplified in order to keep the interest of the audience. How could the actors be heard and understood in their huge theatres? They certainly must have mastered the technique of good speaking. Moreover, they used brass masks whose advantages were twofold: firstly the mask pictured the general mood of the particular actor in a particular scene and secondly, the well-placed voice of the speaker was adequately reinforced (also by use of brass vases, called Echeia, placed between the rows of seats in the auditorium). Without these ingenious auxiliary means it seems unlikely that common folk would have listened with interest to the plays of Aeschylus, Sophocles and Euripides for hours and even days.

Singers should consider that they are using their own God-given instrument—the voice—as a musical instrument which differs from the mechanical instruments in that only the owner and no one else can 'play' it. This instrument has its own sounding board, just like the piano with its wooden sounding board, which is able to amplify the tones. The sounding board in the singer's 'instrument' is the skull and its cavities. The piano sounding board reacts only when the pedal is used; that of the voice only when the sounding breath is able to float undisturbed by obstacles through the throat and mouth. Only then can the sounding breath keep sufficient power to emit tone not only through the open mouth and partly through the nose of the singer, but also cause the skull and its cavities to co-vibrate. This resonance of the skull and its cavities is called head resonance and singers who are able to sing with the use of it enjoy fundamental advantages over others who do not know the secret or are not able to acquire it.

In order to understand the difficulties in the education of the voice as an instrument we must consider the following important facts:

1. The human musical instrument is used without vocal instruction since the first baby cry.
2. Babies learn to use their voice automatically by imitating imperfect models.
3. Whatever the physiological difference between the functions of speaking and singing, the vocal chords are used for both.
4. The beginning voice-student learns to use his instrument in order to 'make music with it' but it is the same instrument which he is accustomed to use automatically; thus he thinks not how to produce the tone but how to make his feelings, wishes and ideas understood. He must first learn to make his voice beautiful, flexible and consistent.

For years students and lecture audiences have asked me why all singers and speakers are not able to use head resonance. The answer is: head resonance functions only under certain conditions, one of which is correct breathing. Most people are accustomed to automatic inhaling and exhaling instinctively, filling only the upper part of the lungs. But singers and especially opera singers, who not only have to fill large halls with their voices but whose voices must carry above the orchestra, need greater quantities of breath. The breath is the raw material which the singer transforms into tone with the vibration of his vocal chords. Although the strength of the voice does not depend exclusively on the power of the breath, there can be no doubt that singers must fill all available cavities, 'storage rooms' so to speak, in order to provide sufficient raw material (breath). It is important for singers to know that singing without adequate quantities of breath will jeopardise their voice sooner or later. And they must be taught to use their breath properly. The idea that good singing is based on good speaking only is basically wrong since speaking in daily communication requires much less breath (besides other differences) than singing. Out-door sports are an important therapy for shallow breathing habits since the exertion demands deeper inhalation.

In his authoritative and most instructive book *The Voice of Neurosis* (Grune & Stratton, New York, 1954), Dr. Paul J. Moses says: 'the breathing capacity of babies does not seem to have limits; it functions ideally—a trait which, unfortunately, will soon be lost . . . If the same child takes singing lessons eighteen years later, it will only be with great difficulty that some of this ideal breathing and phonation is regained.'

Another obstacle in the path of singing with head resonance is the presence of spasms in the throat during tone production. To understand how spasms in the throat and mouth hinder the floating breath, think of the upholstered door in a dentist's office which withholds the sound of the drill from the patients in the waiting room. The self-inflicted hindrance is the most difficult to eliminate since one is so familiar with the automatic 'technique' of speaking learned in infancy. Just as the beginning tennis player uses his wrist instead of his upper arm in his stroke until he is taught better tennis, so the beginning singer tends to use the muscle group

nearest the larynx and mouth until he is taught to use the diaphragm in correct breathing.

It is clear then, that the first task of the voice teacher should be
to repair the instrument and teach the student how to keep it in
good condition. Only when correct breathing is a habit can the
further development of his art proceed in a similar manner to the
advancement of the student of a mechanical instrument.

A teacher who is himself able to sing with head resonance (and
thoroughly understands its use) will successfully teach it to his
students. However, to comfort teachers and students, I want to
emphasise that there are students who automatically sing with
head resonance and that the teacher, relying on his good ear and
good taste, needs only to guide the use and development of the
natural gift.

Obviously, I do not intend to minimise the importance of other
resonances such as that of the chest with which most singers and
teachers are much more familiar.

I was most fortunate to be able to follow closely the artistic
development of Lilli Lehmann and Mattia Battistini and above all,
to learn from their prolonged singing activity the immense signi-
ficance of head resonance. First-rate singers whose careers lasted
more than thirty years were always rare, the last well known were
Lauritz Melchior, who sang for 35 years on stage (and singing
Wagner means much more 'heavy work' than lyrical singing),
and Giovanni Martinelli who sang opera for 36 years. Female
singers usually start at an earlier age but the majority of them have
to stop for physiological reasons in their fifties. Our mechanical
age has brought numerous advantages for outstanding singers, but
there is no doubt that 'modern speeds of transportation aggravate
the situation', as Albert Goldberg comments in his interesting
article 'Today's Opera Voices Short on Longevity'. There will
be fewer singers whose voices will escape early deterioration, because of modern conditions. The ability to use head resonance

will therefore be of increasing importance to counteract the bad effect on the voice of repeated sudden climatic change, constant change of conductors and cast and so forth. There are, nevertheless, all over the world some singers who enjoy a long career owing it mainly to their head resonance.

By way of comparison, there is a decided difference between actors who can only appear in films with the microphone near their mouth, and such actors as Laurence Olivier, Alec Guiness, Richard Burton and others who can, at will, be also stage actors. In addition to other artistic abilities it is the use of head resonance which is mainly responsible for their versatility.

It must be emphasised that the ability (I would even say art) to use head resonance is no competition to the microphone, the ingenious invention which is vital to our mass communications media and electronic industries. But sleeping pills have not replaced natural sleep, nor has the motor vehicle caused our legs to fall off from disuse. Just so, the mechanical microphone and its attending apparatus cannot replace the function of the singer's own microphone—head resonance which provides the singer with a blessing which no amount of engineering genius can invent: beauty, protection and nearly everlasting durability.